*Garden Way's*

# Growing & Saving
# VEGETABLE SEEDS

Marc Rogers

*Illustrated by Polly Alexander*

GARDEN WAY PUBLISHING
CHARLOTTE, VERMONT 05445

*Printed in the United States*
*First printing, May 1978*

Library of Congress Cataloging in Publication Data

Rogers, Marc.
  Growing & saving vegetable seeds.

  Bibliography:  p.
  Includes index.
  1. Vegetable seed.    2. Vegetable gardening.
I.  Title.
SB324.75.R63        635'.04'21        78-6672
ISBN 0-88266-132-9

# Contents

## THE VEGETABLES

### MONOCOTYLEDONAE

### DICOTYLEDONAE

CHAPTER 1

# Why Raise Seeds?

A sneeze several years ago started me along the circuitous route toward growing seeds to save.

I had heard the arguments against growing seeds for so long that I believed them all. Don't grow seeds, the garden books say. Then come some arguments that boil down to one point, and that is that you and I really aren't smart enough. Our grandfathers, their fathers, and generations back to those who first swung out of a tree raised their own, but the plain truth is that the human line has petered out a bit, and you and I aren't capable of growing our own.

Then comes the final argument: Seeds are so cheap.

I won't argue that seeds at almost any price are a bargain. Think for a moment of man building a kit that would include all of the parts and the directions for building a celery plant, think of him being able to do this—and then offer it so that the entire package, parts, directions, and container, weighs but 1/70,000 of an ounce.

Nature has designed such a kit—a celery seed.

1

But *are* seeds cheap? I hadn't thought of it too much, only realizing that each January my seed bill was bigger, but the garden stayed the same. And noticing that I paid $2 for what I thought was a dollar's worth of peas.

Then came that sneeze. Surprising how it snuck up on me. Surprising how loud it was. Surprising me so that my right hand snapped skyward. My right hand at that moment was holding a few seeds—$3 worth of tiny petunia seeds. The dustlike seeds shot up, then were caught in the gale of the sneeze and scattered to, in this case, the one wind.

Gone, but not forgotten. For that incident started me thinking more about seed costs. My handy calculator soon told me that if I had managed to sneeze away a pound of those petunia seeds, instead of 1/64th of an ounce, my sneeze bill for the day would have been more than $3,000. That's more than gold costs, and it certainly shows that seeds aren't cheap.

I noticed, too, that seed packets were changing. Only infrequently did they tell the number of seeds to be found therein. The price for a packet most often was about 75 cents. And no longer were the packets fat with seed. Some were downright slim, even undernourished, in shape.

Today's prices haven't dropped from those of several years ago when I first began to watch them. The move of prices has been in the opposite direction. A good hybrid tomato seed sells for $3 for 1/32nd of an ounce. I'll save you calculating that and tell you it's $1,536 a pound—and even more expensive than that if you buy by the packet instead of the comparatively large amount of 1/32nd of an ounce.

I had found one good reason for raising and saving seeds. To save money. The day of the nickel packet of seeds was over. It was time I looked for almost-free seeds.

Are there other good reasons for growing and saving seeds?

I immediately thought of a Lebanese family in town. Their grandparents had arrived on Ellis Island years ago, bringing with them little money, only a few clothes, a handful of squash seeds and a headful of recipes for cooking those squash in the most delectable manner. Various grandchildren now are growing what must be the sixtieth generation of those seeds in this country, never giving this squash an opportunity to exercise its promiscuous habit of crossing with any other member of its not-so-immediate family.

Here was another reason for growing and saving seed. To preserve and perpetuate varieties that could die out. Look at a seed catalog of ten or twenty years ago, and compare varieties of seeds with current offerings. Many have been dropped, some for good reason, others because it doesn't pay to carry too many varieties. Perhaps one of those dropped was exactly what you wanted, because of its taste or keeping qualities or looks. If you had saved seed, you could have continued a variety now forgotten. The decision on your choice would not be entirely in the hands of the seed companies.

Many good old heirloom strains, no longer offered commercially, have already been lost. Some of the good vegetables we enjoy today—the Royalty bean and Clemson Spineless okra are examples—are still available to us because one family nurtured and handed down the seed for generations. Once a variety dies out, it cannot be retrieved.

If you have seed of a special, obscure, unusual, or heirloom vegetable variety, you—and many other people—might some day be glad that you kept the strain vital by planting and saving it.

If you raise and save seed, you are producing seed for *your* garden, and, by careful selection over several generations of plants, you can produce plants best suited to *your* climate and *your* gardening conditions. No one else but you can do this. Flavor, pest and disease resistance, early bearing, and size are among the many characteristics that can be enhanced by judicious selection over a period of years.

A few seasons ago seeds became scarce as the number of home gardeners spurted. Something like this could happen again in the future, caused by a truck strike, blizzard, postal mix-up, or failure of crops. If you have raised and saved seeds, such an event will not hamper your gardening activities one bit. In fact if you have raised more seeds than you need, as most of us do, you will be able to help your neighbors in a most meaningful way.

If you have a keen eye as you observe, evaluate, select, and compare your plants, you may find something new and valuable. The chances may be against it, but good new strains of plants have been found and are being found, some by plant breeders and a few by observant every-day gardeners. One such person was a turn-of-the-century seed grower, C. N. Keeney of New York State, who is credited with originating nine new varieties of beans, among them the Burpee's Stringless Green Pod, still listed in the Burpee catalog and credited as having the "finest flavor."

There's one benefit on which you will have to put a value. I can't. Let's say you first attempt something easy—saving peas. The year that you plant those, you will put them in the ground with a little extra care. They'll get the choice compost for encouragement. You'll spend a minute or two longer with them each time you cultivate around them. And, sure enough, they'll taste a bit sweeter than any other peas you raise that year. There'll be a deeper satisfaction in growing them. What's that worth to you?

The final reason for raising seed: To prove to those writers of gardening books that the human strain hasn't weakened to the point where it is incapable of growing vegetable seeds. Grandpa was a smart old codger, but not that smart. Maybe he just grew seeds for saving because no one told him he couldn't.

## Satisfying Hobby

Seed-growing can be a satisfying, fascinating hobby, and you can select your own level of involvement. Perhaps that will be at the easy level of growing your own peas and beans for seeds. Perhaps you'll try selecting your best carrots to replant the following spring. Perhaps you'll find a way to grow cauliflower seed without the use of a greenhouse, and write to tell me how to do it. Be assured. You won't outgrow this hobby, no matter how much you experiment, how much you learn.

If you have any doubts about this, look at some of our historic figures of the past—Jefferson is a good example—who found a lifetime of satisfaction from experimenting in this area. Or look at what some of today's professionals in the field are attempting. A single example is the present effort to give other plants the ability of many legumes to host soil organisms which change the nitrogen in the air to a form that can be used by the plant.

## Arguments Against Growing Seeds

You will face discouraging arguments about raising seeds both in what you read and in your conversations with other gardeners. Such as these:

*You can't save the seeds of hybrids, because they won't produce true in the next generation.* True, but there are many open-pollinated varieties that were growing successfully long before the hybrids were developed. This is not an attempt to belittle the contribution of hybrids. Many of them are more vigorous, resist diseases, and produce more food per plant than do the open-pollinated varieties. But this doesn't mean that you can't find hardiness, top flavor, and great satisfaction in the varieties that you can raise for seed.

*It is difficult for the gardener to isolate varieties and strains to avoid unwanted cross-pollination.* And this is one of the reasons why the commercial seed-growing industry has moved westward into dry areas where there are fewer wild or garden varieties that may cross with the crop being grown for seed. Cross-pollination can be a major problem if the gardener works in the midst of other gardens where he has no control over what is being grown around him. This at best is a delightful challenge to the gardener, and at worst may limit the breadth of his seed-growing activities.

*Unwanted cross-pollination and faulty selection of seed plants results in the gradual deterioration or "running out" of the seed. If and when it does, buy fresh seed.*

Raising and saving seeds is not for everyone. The gardener whose only aim is to grow as much food as possible may not be interested. The gardener to whom the height of adventure is trying a new variety of tomato may back away. But the gardener who enjoys a challenge, who likes to try something different, who wonders about the "why" of the plant world—this person should try raising seeds. There will be failures and problems and disappointments, but these will only make his successes the sweeter.

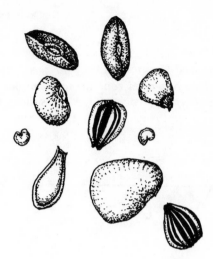

CHAPTER 2

# What Is a Seed?

A seed is more, much more, than it appears to be. The hard, dry, distinctively shaped particles that we plant in our gardens are really dormant embryos, tiny, already formed plants encased in a protective coating. While we may think of seeds as a beginning, they are really links between generations of plants, vehicles for both the survival of the plant species and the spread of new life.

This one-chapter course in botany, while ignoring many fine points, exceptions, and variations, will give you the general idea of the process by which a seed is formed. This is necessary for a clear understanding of what you hope to accomplish when you save seed from your garden plants.

## Parts of a Seed

Difficult as it may be, imagine all the essential rudiments of a plant—leaves, stem, and root—encapsulated in a tiny, uniform fragment of life. That is indeed what each seed contains. Take

*The well-timed miracle of the seed. First, the seed is planted. Next it thrusts down its root tip and unfolds its rudimentary leaves. Then those leaves reach above the soil as the roots expand. Finally the tiny plant produces its first true leaves.*

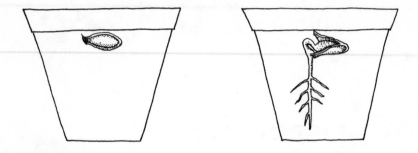

the seed of a snap bean, for example. Soak the seed in water for a few hours and slip off the hard outer seed coat. It is easier to see, in the large seed of the bean, what is true of all seeds. There, compressed within that hard outer coating, are a set of rudimentary leaves called *cotyledons*, a bud that appears as a tiny tuft of leaves, a stem from which both cotyledons and bud arise, and—on the opposite end of the stem—a root tip.

Every seed has within it a reserve supply of carbohydrates, fat, protein, and minerals to nourish the dormant encapsulated plant. Some seeds, like the snap bean, lima bean, watermelon, and pumpkin, have thick, fleshy cotyledons (first leaves), which store nourishment. In other kinds of seeds, the young plant's food supply is found, not in the leaves, but in the *endosperm*, a material that occupies the remaining space within the seed coat, beside and around the embryonic plant. The endosperm is floury in some kinds of plants; in others it is oily, waxy, or hard. Buckwheat and most cereal seeds, for example, contain a floury endosperm.

Far from being lifeless, seeds are actually living, resting plants in an embryonic state. Although the life processes of the seed are operating at a very low ebb, they are operating. Seeds carry

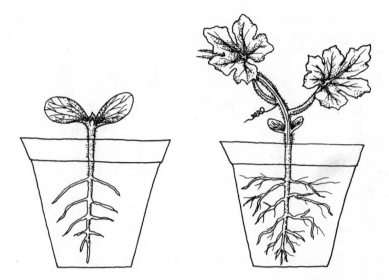

on internal metabolic activity while they are dormant. They absorb moisture from the air. The stored food of the endosperm or the cotyledons combines with that moisture to form a soluble, and therefore usable, form of plant food for the resting embryo.

## Kinds of Seeds

Although there is a great variety of size, shape, texture, and hardness in the seeds that flowering plants produce, most embryonic plants (seeds) follow the same general design. They have two primary leaves with root tip and stem and sometimes with endosperm enclosed in a protective covering. Plants that have two cotyledons—the largest group of seed-bearing plants —are called *dicots*.

A smaller group, termed *monocots*, produces seed containing only one cotyledon. As you've probably noticed, the large family of grasses, to which corn, rye, and other grains belong, sends up a single shoot when the seed germinates, rather than

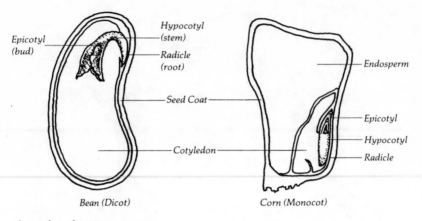

*Epicotyl (bud)*

*Hypocotyl (stem)*

*Radicle (root)*

*Seed Coat*

*Cotyledon*

*Endosperm*

*Epicotyl*

*Hypocotyl*

*Radicle*

*Bean (Dicot)*                    *Corn (Monocot)*

*A seed and its many parts.*

the paired leaves that form on most other vegetable crops. Onions, too, are in this group.

While some seeds will germinate at any time, there are many others that follow an internal time clock, a rhythm that insures —as nearly as it is possible to do so—that when the seed does germinate, conditions will be right for its growth. Some seeds must undergo cold or freezing temperatures in order to break dormancy. Still others need light to germinate. Lettuce seed may refuse to germinate in hot weather, when chances for the success of the plant are lower than in cool seasons.

If you remember only one fact from this quick crash course in botany, let it be this: Seeds are alive.

CHAPTER 3

# How Seeds Are Formed

More than half the plants that grow on our earth are flowering plants. Many of the flowers are small and inconspicuous, like those of wheat and corn, but the seeds they produce have made possible some of the most influential plant improvements that people have been able to work out.

A flower's purpose in life is to produce seed. Although flowers differ tremendously in color, size, and complexity, each is uniquely equipped to form seed. Two parts of the blossom are essential to seed production: The *stamen* or pollen-bearing part of the plant, and the *carpels*, which receive the pollen and nurture the future seeds. The long, thin stalk of the stamen is called the *filament*. The pollen sacs on the ends of the filaments are *anthers*. The stamen, with its filaments and anthers, is sometimes called the "male" part of the plant. The carpels, or "female" parts, include the *stigma* or pollen-receptive region, the *style*, a long, thin tube leading from the stigma to the ovary, and the *ovary* itself, a cavity containing one or more ovules (eggs). The whole organ composed of an ovary with ovules topped by a style and stigma is called a *pistil*.

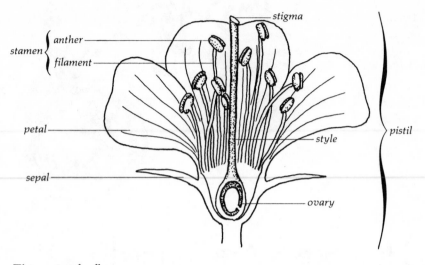

*The parts of a flower.*

Seed is formed from the union of a ripe ovule and a grain of fertilizing pollen. When a pollen grain lands on the stigma of a receptive species, perhaps carried there by the wind or a bee, it begins to grow, putting forth a long thread of living matter that grows down through the style, enters the ovary and penetrates an ovule, where it enters the embryo sac. The two cells —that of the pollen and that of the "egg"—unite to form a single living cell, called a *zygote*, which then has the power to multiply. The single-celled zygote—much divided and enlarged and finally matured—becomes the embryo of the new plant, that rudimentary leaf–bud–stem–root that is somehow all there in even the tiniest of seeds. The ovule develops into the *seed coat*.

And what about the *endosperm*, that layer of nourishment for the new plant? How is it formed? There's an answer for that question too; at least botanists know what the process is. The why of the intricate impulses that cause these things to happen is still an unanswered question. Although the grain of pollen, when first formed, was a single cell, it has usually split to form two cells by the time it reaches the stigma. One of these cells, you will remember, unites with the embryo sac of the ovule to form the zygote, which will grow into an embryonic plant. The second cell joins with other minute parts of the embryo sac—called *nulcei*—to form the endosperm, after much division and redivision of cells.

The *ovary*, usually containing multiple seeds, develops into the fruit, which we sometimes call a vegetable, that is often the end product of our gardening efforts. Examples are tomatoes and peppers.

Once the embryo plant within the seed has formed completely, growth stops and the seed enters a period of dormancy during which, as mentioned earlier, the plant consumes minute amounts of energy from the stored endosperm, just enough to keep it on "holding." The seed is alive, barely, but it should grow or develop no further until it is planted.

CHAPTER 4

# Annuals, Biennials, and Perennials

## Annuals

Let's start with the easiest to grow, the annuals, those garden plants that can be grown from seed to maturity and then allowed to go to seed themselves, all within the span of one growing season.

Some plants that are grown as annuals in the average North American garden—tomatoes, peppers, lima beans, cotton and castor beans—are actually perennials in their native tropics.

Other annuals, such as spinach, lettuce, wheat, and some rye plants, may survive a mild winter after fall planting, and produce seed in the spring as if they were biennials. Hardy annuals will produce more seed in mild-winter areas when planted in the fall and carried through the winter than when matured in extremely hot summer weather.

With these exceptions, annuals will bear seed the same year they are planted. They need no special pampering, only to be given their normal cultural requirements and to be planted early enough in the spring to give them time to ripen seed before they are killed by frost.

The common vegetables that are annuals are bean, broccoli, Chinese cabbage, corn, cucumber, eggplant, lettuce, muskmelon, pea, pepper, pumpkin, most radishes, spinach, squash, and tomato. One of these is the best starting point for most gardeners wishing to raise seeds.

If you are noted for a certain crop, try that one. Peas are a good example, or snap beans. Tomatoes are, too, though remember that hybrids should not be grown for seeds.

To make your chances of success even greater, make your choice from among the self-pollinating annuals—snap beans, lettuce, peas, tomatoes.

As you know, *self-pollinated* means pollination occurs within each flower, and not from either other plants or other flowers on the same plant. (More about this in the next chapter.)

*The fall harvest.*

The reason for choosing one of these? These vegetables do not depend on either the wind or the insect world for assistance in pollinating. While insects sometimes do pollinate some of these, the problem of isolation, or separation of varieties to avoid crosses, is practically eliminated.

# Biennials

Raising seed from biennial plants takes a little more persistence. These vegetables bear their edible crop the season they are planted, waiting until the second season to flower, produce seed, and wither away. Where cold in winter is severe, most biennials must be dug up in the fall and replanted in the spring. Some of them can be left in the garden and covered with a blanket of hay or leaves, and they will survive to grow seeds.

Without a doubt you have thought of these biennials as annuals. They include beet, Brussels sprouts, cabbage, carrot cauliflower, celeriac, celery, onion, parsley, parsnip, rutabaga, salsify, Swiss chard, and turnip.

During their second growing season, most biennials flower in the spring and ripen their seed in midsummer or late summer. The typical biennial flower grows on a sturdy stalk that originates in the root or leafy crown of the plant. Stalk formation may not be seen but is well under way by winter after the plant's first growing season. For a plant to form a good strong seed stalk, the following conditions are usually necessary:

1. The plant should be a mature, well-developed specimen. Small or immature plants may not form seed even if chilled.

2. A chilling period of at least 30–60 days, with temperatures no higher than 40°–50° F.

3. Moderate weather prevailing during the period of new spring growth in the parent plant.

The biennials pose a new complication for the seed-grower. He must carry the vegetable over the winter in good enough condition so that it will flower and produce seed the following year.

This can be as simple as salsify, so hardy that a covering of hay or leaves will protect the roots in the garden during the worst of winters in the North, to cauliflower, which in the North will not survive outdoors, and cannot be stored in a root cellar, so must be grown one season outdoors, transplanted into a cold frame or greenhouse for the winter, then moved out again in the spring.

## Perennials

Perennials return each year, growing from a strong root that lives over the winter. Most perennials planted from seed will begin to produce seed themselves a year or two after planting. Rhubarb and asparagus are the most frequently grown perennial garden vegetables.

CHAPTER 5

# Pollination

The little boy had been well satisfied that storks brought babies. But his father felt the son should know more than that, so gave him a detailed account of the Facts of Life.

The next day the boy's pal asked him where babies came from. "The stork brings them," the boy explained. "But you should have heard the wild story my Dad tried to tell me last night."

Beginning seed-growers may share with that boy a desire for simplicity regarding pollinating, but will find nature unco-operative. There is not one simple method, but many. There are the self-pollinating flowers, those that cross with other flowers on the same plant, those that cross with others of the same variety, those that cross with other varieties, and many that cross with weeds. The variations seem endless. The seed-grower must understand the pollination process of each of the vegetables he raises for seeds or his efforts will fail.

# Self-Pollination

A good starting point for understanding pollination (as well as for growing seeds) was suggested in the previous chapter. It's the self-pollinating vegetables. All have complete flowers, containing both male and female parts.

Such vegetables as these can be grown fairly close to other varieties of the same vegetable without fear of crossings which result in unwanted variations from the parent plant.

The following grains and vegetables are generally self-pollinating:

| | | | |
|---|---|---|---|
| Pea | Soybean | Oats | Wheat |
| Snap bean | Cowpea | Tomato | Lettuce |
| Barley | Endive | | |

Self-pollination results when the pollen of a flower fertilizes that same flower.

# Cross-Pollination

*Cross-pollination* results when the pollen from one flower fertilizes another flower, either on the same or on another plant. The pollen is carried either by the wind or by insects, usually bees.

Within this group there are many variations. Some cabbages, for example, have complete flowers, but flowers that are self-sterile, and thus require the pollen from other plants. This means, to the seed grower, that he must not plan to grow cabbage seed by carrying over just a single plant to set out in the spring.

The complete flower, then, is found on vegetables that self-pollinate as well as cross-pollinate. It is found in the orchard (apple, peach, pear and plum) as well as in the vegetable garden. (Bean, carrot, celery, eggplant, radish, sweet potato, tomato, pepper, and okra are but a few of them.)

## Incomplete Flowers

There are other flowers with functional stamens and non-functional pistils (called *staminate* or *male flowers*), and flowers with nonfunctional stamens and functional pistils (*pistillate* or *female flowers*). Both of these are called *incomplete* flowers.

When a plant has *both* staminate and pistillate flowers, it is called a *monoecious* plant (sweet corn, cucumber, cantaloupe, squash, pumpkin, and watermelon, as well as many members of the nut families, including chestnuts, filberts, pecans, and walnuts). When those staminate and pistillate flowers occur on different plants, they are called *dioecious* plants. Holly is probably the best known of this group, which also includes asparagus, date, and persimmon. Spinach produces male plants, female plants, and plants with both male and female flowers.

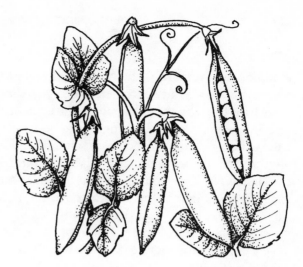

CHAPTER 6

# Selection of Seed

Selection of seed is the heart of any garden seed-saving program. If you are careful in choosing the seed that you save from your garden, you can not only perpetuate and multiply your garden plants, but also improve and refine them. Naturally, you will want to save seed from your best plants, since superior plants are more likely to produce seed that will grow into another generation of plants with the same desirable characteristics.

If you intend to save garden seed, don't wait until fall to decide on the parent plants. Watch your plants throughout the growing season, keeping in mind the qualities you want most to encourage. To decide on the best plants, you need to know how they performed all season long.

## Consider the Whole Plant

It is the *whole plant*, rather than an isolated individual fruit, that you should consider in making your selection. For example, in choosing a tomato plant, you would want to save seed from a vine that bore many excellent fruits, not simply from one lone huge fruit that caught your eye on the edge of the patch.

The luscious, early-bearing plant that you'd choose first to eat is the one from which you should save seed. That's not always easy to do, especially when the family is clamoring for the first sweet corn, or when you haven't eaten a fresh tomato for seven whole months and the first one is ready and waiting on the vine. Many gardeners who regularly save seed see enough of an improvement in the plants grown from seed they select, to make the sacrifice worthwhile. If you're not particularly set on cultivating an early strain, though, preferring to select only for flavor or some other quality, then of course you can go ahead and feast on those very first fruits of your vegetable patch.

If you're saving seed of root crops—carrots, beets, turnips, rutabaga, celeriac, parsnip, salsify—which are biennials, you'll need to dig and store the roots over winter unless you live in an area where winters are mild. Select the roots for desirable qualities as you pack them away, and then re-select from the stored roots in the spring, choosing for your prime seed stock those that have remained in good shape throughout the storage period. Persons saving potatoes for planting will make the same choices.

You'll have the best luck with cabbage and other brassicas if you'll let them grow to eating size, or nearly so, before they go through the winter in your garden or cold cellar. Plants that winter over in an immature state don't always flower and set seed reliably the following spring.

## More Than One

If you intend to save seed from your vegetables each year, experts advise that you'd be wise to keep seeds from more than one plant of the same variety, even if you only need a few seeds,

*Beans to be saved for seeds.*

so that you maintain a broader genetic base for your garden improvement experiments. This is especially true of corn.

There are two exceptions to this rule. Self-pollinated vegetables such as beans and peas are inbred by nature, and thus all seeds could be saved from one plant without fear of deterioration. If healthy, productive plants are chosen, the seeds should improve in quality. The second exception is with squashes and pumpkins. Seeds from one squash or pumpkin can be saved without any change in the quality of the plants the following year.

## What About Hybrids?

Home gardeners are generally advised not to save seeds from hybrid crops. The offspring of hybrid plants, especially corn, are sometimes sterile. When they do bear fertile seed, that seed will produce plants unlike the parent plant. The product of a cross between hybrid plants often reverts to resemble one of its ancestors.

Since the reason for growing hybrid seed is usually the exceptional vigor to be found in the first generation after the cross, there would be little to gain from breeding hybrids back in the direction of their parent and grandparent plants. There's certainly no harm in saving hybrid seed, though. If you like to experiment, go ahead and plant those seeds. Don't expect great things of this second generation, but keep your eyes open and you might grow something you would enjoy. You shouldn't *depend* on seed saved from a hybrid crop, though, if you want to be sure of harvesting what you need next year.

It's a good idea to keep records, when saving seed, of the kind and number of plants from which you gathered seed, along with any other pertinent data such as yield or earliness notations for the parent plants. This will help you to evaluate the results of your seed-saving efforts after you have been following the practice for a few years.

# Plant Qualities

There are many good qualities to look for when selecting plants from which to save seed. You'll want to consider at least some of the following characteristics when choosing your parent plants:

1. Flavor
2. Yield
3. Vigor
4. Color
5. Size
6. Storage life
7. Disease resistance
8. Insect resistance
9. Early bearing (fruits, heads, etc.)
10. Late in bolting to seed (lettuce, etc.)
11. Good germination in poor weather
12. Absence of thorns, spines, etc.
13. Seeds—few, small in juicy fruits, large for sunflowers, tender for tomatoes.
14. Texture, tenderness, juiciness
15. Suitability for purpose. For example, a paste tomato should be dry and meaty. Flint corn should dry well. Kraut cabbage should be solid.

CHAPTER 7

# Collecting Seeds

When you have selected the plants from which you intend to save seed, your first step is to identify the chosen plants so that they don't accidentally end up in the soup pot before you've had a chance to harvest the seed you want. Some gardeners tie a bright cloth or yarn to their elite seed-producing vegetables. Others mark the plant with a stake and some go so far as to post a little sign. If more than one family member regularly harvests garden produce, you will want to be sure that the rest of the family knows which plants should not be picked.

## Timing

Your next concern will be to determine the right time to collect the seeds. Seed that is picked too early, before it has had time to mature, will not have had a chance to accumulate enough stored nourishment to get it off to a good start, or even to last it through the winter. Such seed will be likely to be thin and light in weight. It will be less likely to survive storage, to germinate well, or to produce strong seedlings.

So you want your seed to be well ripened before you pick it but not so far along that it rots into the ground or gets blown away by the wind.

Generally speaking, seed-bearing garden plants will fall into one of three groups, depending on how they ripen their fruit:

1. Plants with seeds encased in fleshy fruits, such as tomatoes, eggplants, and peppers. These soft fruits should be allowed to turn fairly ripe, even a bit over-ripe, before seed is collected. The fruits should be slightly soft but they should not be so over-ripe that they begin to heat. It is also important not to allow the fruit to dry around the seed, or it may form a hard covering that will affect the storage life of the seed.

2. Seed crops, such as corn, wheat, beans, and others in which the seed is the edible part of the plant. Such plants usually hold their seeds for some time after they reach maturity, giving you a chance to do your collecting pretty much when you choose, as long as the seed has become thoroughly dry. Mature plants with dry seeds that tend to bend over in wind or rain may be cut and stacked in a dry place to cure and dry further before removing the seed.

3. Plants that shatter readily, scattering ripe seed as soon as it reaches maturity. Lettuce, onions, okra and the cabbage family not only drop their mature seeds promptly as soon as they're dry; they also tend to ripen seed gradually so that a single plant will usually have a good bit of unripe seed hanging on while matured seed is falling off.

To be sure of catching a good seed crop from such plants, you must either inspect them daily and collect ripe seed in small amounts in a paper bag as it becomes ready, or tie a ventilated paper bag over the seed head. The seed that will collect in the bag may still contain some immature specimens, but these can usually be winnowed out by pouring the seed from one container to another in a breeze.

Some plants in this group, especially those of the cabbage family, will need staking to support the seed stalk.

When collecting any seeds, try to do the job on a dry, sunny day after dew has evaporated. Although most of the seeds that you'll harvest in the fall will not be hurt by the low temperature of a light frost, the frost *can* cause an accumulation of moisture that will lower seed quality.

To prevent confusion, label each batch of seeds as soon as possible after collecting, especially if you're saving more than one variety of a species, such as several varieties of tomato or peppers or several different members of the cabbage family, whose seeds are much alike.

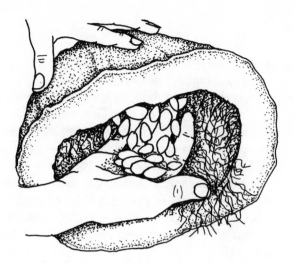

CHAPTER 8

# Extracting and Drying Seeds

Your first job, after collecting seed-containing fruits such as tomatoes, peppers, squash, and melons, is to separate the seed from the pulp. Scrape out the seedy part of the fruit and save the rest of the over-ripe flesh for your hens or put it in the compost pile. It's a good idea to let the tomato seeds and pulp ferment for three or four days, to help control bacterial canker. To do this, spoon the seedy tomato pulp into a jar, add a quarter-cup of water, and watch, over the next few days, as the lightweight pulp and worthless seeds rise to the top and the heavier, good seeds sink to the bottom.

Some gardeners allow cucumber and melon seeds to ferment too, using the same procedure. Or you can fork out the seeds and wash them.

For squash and pumpkins, separate the seeds from the pulp, wash them thoroughly to remove all traces of vegetable matter and spread them out to dry. Large seeds should dry for five to six days. Smaller ones may be ready in three or four days.

Peas, beans, soybeans, and limas are usually removed from the dry pods by threshing. Don't be TOO rough on these seeds, though. Internal injuries to the seed are more likely with machine processing, but they CAN happen when force is used to remove seeds from their husks. Damage to the seed may not be noticeable but if the embryonic stem or root is bruised, the seed may germinate poorly or produce stunted seedlings.

Seed of lettuce, sunflowers, dill, and others that are picked dry may be shaken through a screen of hardware cloth to sift out chaff.

Further removal of undesirable lightweight seeds and stem and leaf parts, as well as pulp, may be accomplished by floating them off. When you put the seeds in water, the chaff, "dud" seeds and pulp will rise to the top and the good seeds will sink to the bottom. Seeds other than tomatoes that you treat in this way should be promptly spread out for drying.

## Moisture Content

As already mentioned, excess moisture in the seed will lower its quality. Seed that is not dry enough when stored will keep poorly and have a low percentage of germination. A moisture content of over 20 percent will cause bulk-stored seed to heat. Most seeds fare best when stored with a moisture content of 8–15 percent. It is important to thoroughly dry ALL seed that you will store—even already dry-looking seeds like dill and carrot.

You won't be able to tell the exact moisture content of the seed under home conditions, of course, but you *can* give your seeds a long, thorough drying period before you store them, and that should be enough. The important thing to remember is not to package any harvested seed until it has had at least a few days of further air drying after being removed from the plant. The larger the seed, the longer the drying period required.

Most seeds, in most climates, will dry adequately for home storage if spread on paper towels or newspapers in an airy place for a week. They should be turned and possibly spread on fresh dry paper (depending on the kind of seed) several times during that period.

If you were forced to collect your seed during damp weather, or if you live in a humid climate, you might want to use gentle heat to dry some of your seeds like corn and other grains. Such heat must be regulated, though, so that it *never* rises above 110° F., and 90° F. is preferable. Too-rapid drying can cause shrinking and cracking of the seed and formation of a hard, impervious and undesirable seed coat.

A far safer method of hastening the drying process is to spread the seed in the sun, on screens or on a flat roof or pavement, for a day or two of more intensive drying.

CHAPTER 9

# Storing Seeds

Now that you've grown, selected, picked, and dried your seeds, it's time to store them. Improperly dried seeds may deteriorate drastically over the winter. If you're counting on home-saved seed for your spring plantings, or trying to carry on an heirloom strain of a certain vegetable, the loss of a year's crop of seed can be disastrous.

Seeds, you remember, carry on their basic life processes even while dormant, but at a very low rate. The moisture they absorb from the air combines with stored nourishment to form a soluble food, which then combines with oxygen from the air to release carbon dioxide, water, and heat.

Since your seeds are exchanging elements and gases with the atmosphere while they are dormant, your aim in storing them, then, should be to confine those exchanges to the minimum necessary to sustain life in the seed. That means avoiding any stimulation that would encourage the seed to speed up its metabolism, or that would deteriorate the embryo. So your stored seeds must be protected from moisture and heat, as well as from animals and insects that would like to eat them.

# Moisture

Let's consider moisture first. As mentioned above, the presence of moisture triggers the formation of soluble compounds in the plant. Too much moisture in the air will cause the seed to burn up its stored food at too fast a rate, producing excess heat which further lowers the seed's germination ability.

How much dampness is too much? Seeds differ, according to their variety, in their ability to absorb water from the air, even under the same conditions of temperature and humidity. Beans, peas and cereals (including corn) should contain no more than 13 percent moisture for safe storage. Soybeans should have a little less—12.5 percent, and peanuts and most other vegetables even less moisture—around 9 percent, with 4–6 percent being considered ideal for long-term storage.

According to seed expert Dr. James Harrington, each 1 percent reduction in seed moisture, under 14 percent but not below 5 percent, doubles the life expectancy of most vegetable seeds. Lowering the moisture content below 1–2 percent impairs the viability of the seed. You're not likely to get your seeds that dry unless you apply artificial heat. Even though we home gardeners have no way of accurately determining a seed's moisture content, we can use these figures as a guide.

Once the seed has been dried for storage, it should be kept as dry as possible. If seeds are allowed to become damp after the initial dryng, they will lose some of their longevity, even if redried. Sealed, moisture-proof containers such as cans and jars are the best places to keep your seeds, but only if the seed is good and dry before it is put away. Damp seeds, stored in covered containers, deteriorate faster than dry ones in more open storage.

# Temperature

Storage temperature also affects the keeping quality of seeds. Most seeds can tolerate cold and even freezing conditions that would kill the parent plant, sometimes as low as 0° F., as long as they are thoroughly dry. Excess moisture in a seed that is subjected to freezing temperatures may freeze and damage the seed.

Dr. Harrington has found that—at 70 percent relative humidity or lower—it is possible to double the life of the seed for each 9° F. (5° C.) decrease in temperature within the range of 32° F. and 112° F. (0° and 44.5° C.)

It follows, then, that *heat*—especially when combined with high humidity—is the enemy of seed quality. High temperatures not only speed up the seed's rate of internal chemistry; they also promote activity of fungi, molds, bacteria and insects that further impair the seed's viability by adding heat from their respirations and sometimes by excreting chemicals or other by-products that harm the embryo or soften the seed coat.

Molds and fungi thrive in 13–16 percent moisture at temperatures of 85°–95°. They slow down at 70° and barely exist at 50°. Different bacteria thrive at different temperatures, but all of them need a moisture content of 18 percent or so to do much damage. So, to discourage these microorganisms, keep your stored seeds dry and cool.

# Insects

Invasive insects may be kept out by storing seeds in tightly closed containers. If insect eggs are already present in seeds, they may be discouraged by maintaining a temperature no higher than 40°–50° F., at which most insects that would be likely to affect the seed would be relatively inactive.

You can see, then, that the viability of the seed, far from being an absolute prediction, depends heavily on conditions of storage— not only during the first year, but throughout the life of the seed. Onion seed, for example, usually considered to be short-lived, has been kept up to twelve years when dry and well sealed, but goes bad in a few months when stored at high temperatures in a damp place.

# Points to Remember

In summary, for best results with your stored garden seeds, you will want to do the following:

1. Store only thoroughly dried seed.

2. Don't allow seed to become damp after the initial drying.

3. Keep storage temperature as low as possible, preferably between 32° and 41° F.—not freezing, but cold enough to retard the seed's enzyme activity.

4. Keep the storage area as dry as possible, especially if the temperature is near freezing or—as may be the case in warm climates—near 70°.

5. Label all containers with variety, date, and any other pertinent information about the strain you're saving.

6. If you do keep seed in envelopes, store the whole collection in a tightly covered lard can, large mayonnaise jar (often available at restaurants), or other sealed container.

7. Peas and beans are best stored in bags rather than airtight containers.

8. If you keep seeds for more than one year, be sure to protect them as much as possible from heat and dampness during the summer.

From this description, you can see that an ideal place for storing seed is your refrigerator. If there's any doubt about how dry your seeds are, place the uncapped container in the refrigerator, then cap it after two or three days.

The refrigerator, too, is an excellent place to store those seeds left over from summer gardening activities. Place the envelopes of seeds in a canning jar and cap it.

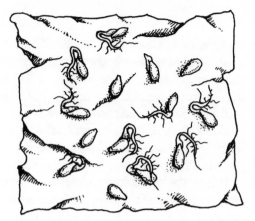

CHAPTER 10

# Testing Seeds

The home seed-grower will want to provide ideal storage conditions for his seed so that germination rates will be high when the seeds are planted, and so that he can carry seeds over for more than one year. For example, he should be able to grow a supply of carrot seeds that will last for several years, having gone to the trouble of spending two years in getting the supply. In this way he can make more profitable use of both his land and time.

## Germination Test

The sure test of his success in storing seeds is the *germination test*. It can be made indoors, before the regular growing season, and thus you avoid the possibly unprofitable use of land in testing the seed.

It's good to test 100 seeds at one time, although lesser amounts can be used. Place several sheets of paper towel on a flat metal surface (a cookie sheet is ideal) and dampen them. Place the seeds on these damp sheets, spacing them rather than leaving them in a clump. Cover them with several more damp sheets of paper toweling. Keep moist, but not so wet that there are puddles. Some seeds such as radishes will germinate in as little as three days, but many will take as much as a week, and some herb seeds take even longer. Be guided by the directions for growing the particular vegetable.

When the seeds have sprouted, make a count of the success. It is here that the use of 100 seeds saves mental work, since it means that the number of seeds germinated is the percentage of germination. If 90 seeds are found germinated, the percentage is 90. If some other amount of seeds is used, divide the number of seeds germinated by the total number tested, and the result is the percentage of germination. (Fifty seeds tested, 45 germinated: Divide 45 by 50 and the answer is .90 or 90 percent.)

The answer you get can be useful in two ways:

1. It tells you whether your seeds are worth planting.
2. If they are, it gives you an indication of how thickly you should plant them, with a heavier planting indicated if the percentage is low.

## Getting Started

You have now completed the basic reading on growing and saving seeds. School's out. It's recess time. It's time to get into the garden, to make mistakes and learn from them, to grow and harvest your own seeds, and experience the rich sense of satisfaction that is in store for you.

The remainder of this book deals with growing specific vegetables for seeds. You would expect, perhaps, that it would be written from A to Z, beginning with asparagus, and ending with that prolific friend of all gardeners, the zucchini.

Instead, it's broken down by those various botanical families with the unpronounceable names. Why? Simply because it is easier to understand about growing seeds if all members of a family are considered together. There's much in common, for example about growing cabbages and broccoli and Brussels sprouts, so much of the material doesn't have to be repeated if they are grouped.

Remember, don't be afraid to wander back into the schoolroom pages occasionally. You'll need that basic information.

# THE
# VEGETABLES

# Table
# of Information

| Vegetable | Page | Life Cycle for Seeds | Seed Viability (Years) | How Pollinated | Need Isolation |
|---|---|---|---|---|---|
| Lima Bean | 91 | Annual | 3 | Self | Limited |
| Muskmelon | 121 | Annual | 5 | Insect | Yes |
| New Zealand Spinach | 65 | Annual | 5 | Wind | Yes |
| Okra | 93 | Annual | 2 | Self | No |
| Onion | 53 | Biennial | 1–2 | Insect | Yes |
| Parsley | 101 | Biennial | 2 | Insect | Yes |
| Parsnip | 102 | Biennial | 1–2 | Insect | Yes |
| Pea | 86 | Annual | 3 | Self | Limited |
| Pepper | 106 | Annual | 4 | Self | Limited |
| Popcorn | 48 | Annual | 1–2 | Wind | Yes |
| Potato | 109 | Annual | | Self | No |
| Pumpkin | 116 | Annual | 5 | Insect | Yes |
| Radish | 81 | Annual | 5 | Insect | Yes |
| Rhubarb | 56 | Perennial | | See listing | No |
| Rutabaga | 79 | Biennial | 5 | Insect | Yes |
| Salsify | 126 | Biennial | 2 | Self | No |
| Soybean | 92 | Annual | 3 | Self | Limited |
| Spinach | 62 | Annual | 5 | Wind | Yes |
| Squash, Summer | 111 | Annual | 5 | Insect | Yes |
| Squash, Winter | 111 | Annual | 5 | Insect | Yes |
| Swiss Chard | 62 | Biennial | 4 | Wind | Yes |
| Tomato | 107 | Annual | 4 | Self | Limited |
| Turnip | 78 | Annual | 5 | Insect | Yes |
| Watermelon | 121 | Annual | 5 | Insect | Yes |

# MONOCOTYLEDONEAE

The monocotyledons are plants with only one seed leaf. The monocotyledons include the members of the grass family and the lily family.

## *GRAMINEAE*

## Grass Family

The members of this family are found throughout the world, and they include all of our cereals, the grasses of our lawns and pastures, the treelike bamboos, the sugar cane that produces so much of our sugar—and many of our weeds.

The most popular member of this family found in our vegetable gardens is corn, one of the New World's greatest contributions.

Don't be afraid to try corn, just because some method of isolation may have to be used to keep the seed from being the result of a cross. It's possible to get both earlier corn and better tasting corn through raising your own seeds. Remember to save for seed the earliest corn that is well developed and has full-grained ears.

**CORN, SWEET** (*Zea mays rugosa*). Annual. Monoecious. Has male (the tassel) and female (silks of ears) flowers on each plant. Wind-pollinated.

Grow only standard (open-pollinated, not hybrid) varieties for seed. These include Golden Midget (yellow, early), Golden Bantam (very sweet, yellow, midseason), Country Gentleman (white, late, and does not have regular rows of kernels), and Stowell's Evergreen (white, late).

Plant in hills (start six seeds per hill, cut back to three plants per hill) or rows (final spacing, 12 inches). Corn is a hungry crop. Furnish plenty of nitrogen to provide the healthy plants that will produce the best seeds. Pollination will be better if planting is in four or more adjacent rows.

To maintain variety purity, ears to be saved for seed must be isolated. Remember that sweet corn will cross with popcorn, flint corn, field corn as well as other varieties of sweet corn.

Three ways to isolate corn are:

1. *By distance*. The distance downwind from the nearest crop of a different variety is most important. A distance of 1,000 feet is recommended for absolute purity, with 250 feet enough if some crossing can be tolerated.

2. *By time*. Make certain the yellow pollen of the other varieties is not being spread when the silk of the corn to be saved is developing. Planting seeds at different times will achieve this.

3. *By isolating the developing ears to be saved*. If there are gardens near yours, this is the only system for the gardener saving seeds. Obtain a supply of bags that are water resistant, but not plastic. One should be placed over each ear to be saved, before the silk can be seen. Tie it in place. You may have to replace bags one or more times as rains disintegrate them.

The tassel, at top, provides the
pollen for the female flowers,
the silks of the ears.

When the pollen can be seen on the tassel, cut off one, remove the bag from an ear on a different plant, and rub the silk with the tassel, then replace the bag. Do this to all ears being saved.

These ears must be protected from unwanted pollen until the silk turns brown. After the bags are removed, tie pieces of woolen yarn around the ears to be saved, to identify them so they will not be gathered and eaten with the rest of the crop.

No matter how modest your demands for seed, treat at least 12–15 ears in this way. This will permit you to rogue (discard) any ears with undesirable traits, and permit you to save seeds with a broad genetic background, and thus avoid unwanted inbreeding.

The gardener should inspect both plants and ears before selecting the ears to be saved. He may wish to save the earliest ears, those from plants with the greatest productivity, or those that show a resistance to very dry conditions. Choosing the fullest, most perfect ears from the earliest bearing plants is recommended.

*Corn to be dried and saved for seeds.*

The ears should be left on the plants about a month later than the remainder of the crop picked for eating. While frost will not damage the seed if the ears are dry and mature, the ears should be picked before hard freezes which could reduce the percentage of germination. Further drying will be necessary. Strip back the husks, then tie or braid several ears together. Hang up in the home. They will dry and at the same time provide a rustic decoration.

Shelling is a splendid winter evening job, and can be done by twisting off the kernels, discarding the ones not completely developed at the end of the ear.

Since corn is usually considered viable for only one to two years, most gardeners will find it wise to raise seed corn annually.

POPCORN (*Zea mays everta*). Follow directions for sweet corn. Remember that there are both hybrid and open-pollinated varieties. Select the latter. Shelling popcorn can injure the hands. Try rubbing ears against one another to make the shelling easier.

# *LILIACEAE*

## Lily Family

The Easter lily and the many other lilies that decorate our flower gardens and homes are in this family, and so are tulips, the tiny lily-of-the-valley, and, most important for vegetable gardeners, the onion and asparagus.

Growing asparagus from seeds takes time, but certainly is possible. Four other members of this family are excellent for the beginner who wishes to experiment with propagation. His success is almost assured. Garlic is foolproof, since no seeds are involved. There are no isolation problems with leeks or chives, and both of these as well as onions are tolerant about storage conditions, with leeks and chives remaining in the ground, and onions needing only a cool, dry storage place, between the first and second year of growth.

**ASPARAGUS** (*Asparagus officinalis*). Perennial. Dioecious (male and female plants). Pollinated by insects.

Raising asparagus from seed requires patience. The crop cannot be harvested for three years, or one more than is required if roots are planted.

Female plants produce red berries which should be gathered in the fall before the first frost. If you are handling small quantities, put the berries in a cloth bag, then crush them by stepping on the bag. Put the mass of seed-pulp into a pail or bowl of water and wash it. The pulp and unwanted light seeds will float to the top and should be discarded. The seeds in the bottom are saved. Dry them for several days by spreading them out and turning them over occasionally. Store them.

Take advantage of advances in the development of varieties by selecting seeds from the rust-resistant Mary Washington or Martha Washington varieties. While bees carry the asparagus pollen, unwanted cross-pollination is rarely a problem for the home gardener because of the few varieties grown. Commercial growers strive for a mile between plantings to assure purity.

**CHIVE** (*Allium schoenoprasum*). Perennial. Pollinated by bees.

The chive makes a deocrative plant for flower gardens and borders with its tiny rose-purple flowers. If flowers and seed are desired, the clumps of chives, of course, cannot be cut back for use in the kitchen. The seed, black and smaller than onion seed, should be harvested when it can be seen, so it will not be lost through shattering. Home gardeners need not worry

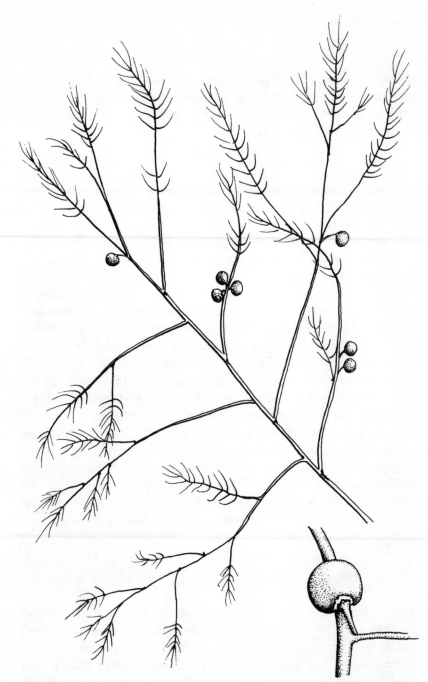

*Berries found on the females of the asparagus plants.*

about undesirable cross-pollination. For harvesting, drying, and storing, see onion. Chives are also easily propagated by division of clumps.

**GARLIC** (*Allium sativum*). Garlic is propagated by dividing the bulbs and planting the individual cloves.

*A garlic bulb divided into cloves for planting.*

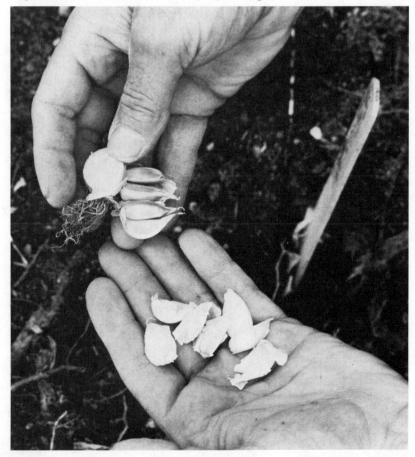

**LEEK** (*Allium porrum*). Biennial. Pollinated by bees. Seeds form second year.

Plants are cultivated as for harvesting the first year. Even in northern climates the plants do not have to be stored, but may be left in the ground. The fall period is an excellent time for the home gardener to rogue out (and eat) the less desirable plants, marking the best for seed production. If you fear the plants will not survive the winter, hill them up with soil, or mulch them with hay or leaves. The second year the individual plants will send up single stalks four to five feet high, each capped with an enormous ball (it's an umbel, composed of hundreds of flowers). Pick the umbels in the fall, and dry them well. The seeds are contained in capsules, and brisk rubbing of the heads is needed to extract the seeds. For other harvesting and drying details, see onion.

*The umbrel of the leek, found in the second year of growth.*

**ONION** (*Allium cepa*). Biennial. Pollinated by bees. Coal black seed forms second year.

To insure purity of variety, onions must be isolated from other varieties in their second year of growth by a distance of a quarter of a mile. However, the gardener need not worry about onions being grown for eating, and thus in the first year of growth, since cross-pollination can of course only occur between flowering plants.

Like onions being grown for home consumption, onions being grown for seed may be started from seeds, sets, or plants. There are two methods of growing them:

1. *Bulb-to-seed*. Most home gardeners will practice this method, growing onions as they would for eating; harvesting and storing them, then replanting them the second year. This gives the gardener an opportunity to select the best onions for planting the following year, and roguing out for eating the ones with such undesirable traits as thick necks or double-onions. This method is used in milder climates, where onions are planted in the fall, harvested the following year, rogued and immediately replanted; as well as in colder areas, where the onions are planted as early in the spring as possible, harvested and rogued in the fall, stored in a cool (32°–40° F.), dry room, then replanted as soon as the ground can be worked in the spring.

2. *Seed-to-seed*. This method means planting seed and letting plants remain in soil through the second year until the seeds are harvested. This reduces the labor involved, and the expense, and is better for those onions that do not store well, such as some of the sweet onions.

When using the first method, the onions should be planted three to four inches apart, in rows three feet apart, the second year. They will send up stalks as high as four feet, capped by

*The umbrel of an onion plant.*

*Onions planted in a wide row save garden space.*

the flowers that produce the seeds. For the second method, thin the onions the second year to three to four inches apart in rows three feet apart.

Some experts advise making a cut down into the top of the onion before replanting it, to hasten the development of the stalk. There is agreement that the larger onion produces more seed.

The heads should be watched from mid-summer. When the black seeds can be seen, start the harvest, cutting off the seed heads and a piece of the stem. Several cuttings may be required, since all seeds will not be ready for harvesting at the same time. Dry the heads, then flail them to remove the seeds. If there is a great deal of debris in the seeds, place them in water, so that the debris will float, while the seeds sink. Do not allow seeds to soak for any length of time. Dry them well and store them.

# DICOTYLEDONEAE

The dicotyledons are plants having two cotyledons or seed leaves. They include most of the common vegetables, except for asparagus, onions (and onion relatives) and corn.

## *POLYGONACEAE*
## Buckwheat or Rhubarb Family

This family includes two members of interest to the home gardener.

One is buckwheat, which may be grown, not to harvest, but to till under to improve the soil. Raising two consecutive crops of buckwheat in a garden is an excellent way to discourage future weed growth. The buckwheat should be turned under not later than the flowering stage to avoid an unwanted future crop.

The second is rhubarb.

**RHUBARB** (*Rheum rhaponticum*). Perennial. Cross-pollinated. Pollinated by insects. Grows best in northern states.

Propagation by division of the crown is strongly recommended, since seeds may not produce plants that are true to the variety.

*The seed stalk of the rhubarb, with its multitude of seeds at the top.*

When planning a bed of rhubarb, select a site that will not interfere with production of annual crops in your garden. Along one side of the garden is preferred. Soil should be prepared by addition of compost, plant foods or manure. In early spring, dig up crown of large parent plant, cut off several chunks for propagating, then replant the original plant. The crowns cut off should be placed about four feet apart, at the same depth as they were found on the parent plant. Six plants will provide ample rhubarb for a family.

Those who wish to try seeds will let the tall center stalk of the plant grow in the summer. Cut off top of stalk when seeds are mature (dry and flaky), separate and dry seeds. Plant them the following spring, thinning them to three to four inches apart when they emerge from the soil. The following spring, select plants wanted for production, and replant them four feet apart in rows six feet apart.

Division of plants is preferable, since it not only assures growing the variety wanted, but also benefits the original plant, which will continue to produce for as many as twenty years. If seeds are not wanted, cut back the seed stalk, to conserve the food supply of the plant, for greater stalk production the following year.

# CHENOPODIACEAE

## The Goosefoot Family

The three members of the goosefoot family described below vary considerably in the work involved in production of seed. Spinach is all too eager to go to seed, and does so the year it is planted. The home gardener must wait two years for seed from Swiss chard, but growing it is relatively easy, since throughout the United States chard is hardy enough to remain in the garden through the winter, in colder climates asking only for a winter coat of mulch for protection. Beets, also biennial, are more difficult to raise for seed since in all but the most moderate of climates, the beets must be gathered and stored for the winter, a trying task very often, when the crop of seeds depends upon success. For the beginner in the growing of seeds, spinach is a good one to try, particularly if the problems of isolation are not insurmountable, while the growing of beet seeds might well be left to the more experienced seedsmen.

**BEET** (*Beta vulgaris*). Biennial. Perfect flowers (have both male and female parts). Cross-pollinated, with extremely light pollen often carried for miles by winds.

The beet produces the familiar rosette of leaves the first year, but the second year produces a seed stalk several feet high. This has branches along which tiny blossoms appear, followed by the beet seed—actually corky seed balls containing seeds enough to produce up to six plants.

Here are two methods for growing beet seeds, and they are used for many of the other biennial vegetables:

1. *Root-to-seed*. The home gardener, particularly in the north, will try this method, growing the beets as if for the kitchen, but planting later in the season, so the beets reach only a moderate size (1″–2″ in diameter) at fall harvesting time. During the growing season, plants with undesirable traits such as poor leaf quality should be pulled, a job that the home gardener will do as he thins, using the thinnings for beet greens.

In the fall, the beets should be pulled. The beets with the most desirable characteristics in color, shape, and size should be saved for seed plants, with the remainder used for eating. The tops of those saved for seed should be cut, but not closer than one inch from the top of the beets. Handle the beets carefully; damaged beets will rot. The home gardener will find that about a half-dozen beets will provide more than enough seeds for his needs,

*These beets are ideal size to save for growing seed.*

but will want to save more than this, in case some of them do not winter well.

Many storage systems are effective. Ideal temperatures are 40°–50° F., or about what is found in many "unheated" basements or root cellars.

Try storing beets in a box, placing a layer of fresh sawdust or sand in the bottom, adding a layer of beets, then another layer of sawdust or sand, and continuing until the box is full. Any storage system should provide some moisture, since a dry, shriveled beet will produce few or no seeds.

In the spring, as soon as the soil can be worked, the beets are set out, crowns barely beneath the soil, and the beets two feet apart in rows three feet apart.

2. *Seed-to-seed*. This method requires less work, the home gardener does not have to worry about storage of the beets, but he does not have the opportunity to select the best roots for propagation, and the method should be used only in mild climates, because beets are not hardy. Seeds are planted in August to September, with the earlier dates in the less mild areas, and for slower-growing varieties. Beets get first-year growth in

the fall, and can be mulched if the gardener knows such protection is needed. In the second year, the beets should be thinned to permit a space of two feet between plants, in rows three feet apart. Most gardeners who have raised beets only for eating and have never seen the second-year growth, are surprised at the height, width and quality of this seed-stalk growth.

Don't attempt seed crops of both beets and Swiss chard the same season. The two will cross (and both will cross with sugar beets). You can of course have first-year crops of both, or a seed crop of one and a first-year crop of the other. Similarly you should not attempt seed crops of more than one variety of beets or Swiss chard the same year. Commercial growers strive for at least a mile distance between seed crops of Swiss chard and beets, or between different varieties of either vegetable. The home gardener, of course, cannot plan for such spaciousness, but he can be comforted by the knowledge that few home gardeners grow either Swiss chard or beets as biennials for seed, and thus the chances of stray air-borne pollen causing unwanted cross-pollination are reasonably small. Because both beet and Swiss chard seeds will remain viable for four or more years if given reasonable treatment, the home gardener can alternate years in growing these two vegetables for seed, and thus always have enough seed for his own use.

When some of the seeds have reached maturity (they will be brown), cut the entire plants at ground level and hang them upside down in a dry, protected area such as a garage or barn. When plants are dry, seed balls are easily stripped by hand from the branches. If only a few beets are being raised for seeds, a convenient method for collecting the seeds is to bend each stalk into a large grocery bag, and strip off the seeds that are brown and mature. This can be repeated when more seeds are mature.

If considerable debris is stripped with the seed balls, the seeds should be cleaned by winnowing. The home gardener may borrow the family wooden salad bowl for this, placing the seed in the bowl on a breezy day, then tossing the seed gently into the air until the lighter trash has blown away.

**SWISS CHARD** (*Beta vulgaris cicla*). Biennial. Perfect flowers (having both male and female parts). Cross-pollinated, by wind.

Swiss chard and beets are very similar, except that Swiss chard is grown for its foliage, while beets are grown for their roots, and, increasingly, for the immature plant, from which both roots and foliage are eaten.

Gardeners throughout the nation can grow Swiss chard by either method listed under beets. There is one difference: Swiss chard is extremely hardy, so there is no need to dig up and store the plants under Method 1. The plants are left in the ground (in extremely cold areas, they can be heavily mulched after the first few frosts), then dug up and transplanted in the spring, at about one foot apart in rows three feet apart. Since the foliage is the part of Swiss chard that is eaten, the gardener need not inspect the roots when roguing out undesirable plants. For this reason Method 2 may be favored by the home gardener. It may be necessary to stake up the stalks as they reach maturity.

Gardeners should be aware that there are both white-stemmed and red-stemmed varieties of Swiss chard. The latter is often called rhubarb chard. While the two taste alike, the rhubarb chard is the choice of many because of its greater ornamental value.

**SPINACH** (*Spinacia oleracea*). Annual. Cross-pollinated. Pollen carried by wind.

The varied curiosities found in the reproductive patterns of plants are well illustrated in the spinach plant. Within one row in your garden may be found four distinct types of plants. The one most desired for both harvesting and seed production is the monoecious plant, having both male and female flowers. Satisfactory, too, are the female plant, having only pistillate flowers, and with foliage that is fine for harvesting, and the

*The late-bolting spinach plants should be saved for growing seeds.*

vegetative male, with staminate flowers and edible foliage. Unwanted and discarded as soon as they are recognized are the extreme male plants, smaller than the others and having staminate flowers and few or no leaves.

The tendency to produce seed early, a desired characteristic in many vegetables, is not wanted in spinach, since the emergence of the seed stalk marks the end of the crop as a desired food plant. Thus the early bolters in your rows should be eliminated, in an attempt to harvest seed that doesn't have this characteristic. Seed should be harvested from among the plants that were the last to bolt.

Seed of this hardy plant is sown in early spring, or, in milder climates, in the fall, with growth completed the following spring. The home gardener will plant in rows two feet apart, and, as the plants reach about six inches in height, he will, in one operation, weed the seed row to insure good growth, rogue out the stunted male plants and any others with an undesirable appearance, and thin the plants to about six inches apart, reserving those thinnings for dinner that evening. At least one more roguing will be needed to eliminate the plants that bolt early.

Spinach bolts when temperatures rise and days grow longer. The flowers may not be recognized as such, since, not having to attract insects, they lack petals. As the plants turn yellow, the seeds are reaching maturity. They may be gathered by pulling the plants, then stripping the seeds from the stalk with your hands.

Maintaining purity of variety in spinach can be nearly impossible in some home gardens, particularly where many varieties are being grown by neighbors and allowed to bolt, thus spreading the dust-like pollen over a vast area. If there are but a few gardeners in an area, perhaps the seed-grower can get the others to agree on a variety all will grow. Otherwise the chances of growing a pure strain are slight. The seed-grower can only rogue out any undesirable plants that grow the following year from the seed he has grown, and expect to purchase commercially grown seed and try again after a few years.

# AIZOACEAE

## Carpetweed Family

This family consists of some 3,000 herbs, and one common vegetable, New Zealand spinach.

**NEW ZEALAND SPINACH** (*Tetragonia expansa*). Annual. Wind-pollinated.

This delightful substitute for spinach will grow and prosper in temperature that would make spinach bolt.

Since the time required to produce seed is long, start plants indoors in a cold frame. Plant out when danger of frost is past, eighteen inches apart in rows three feet apart. Plants bolt slowly. Flowers develop first at bottom of plant, continuing on up the plant.

Plant develops pods containing several seeds each. As they mature, they will shatter. So cut plants and place them on a canvas to cure. They then can be shaken, to dislodge seed, and seed can be gathered.

# CRUCIFERA

## The Mustard or Cabbage Family

The gardener attempting to raise seed of the cabbage family faces two problems:

1. *Isolation*. Broccoli, Brussels sprouts, cabbage, cauliflower, kale, and kohlrabi will cross if any of them are *flowering* at the same time. The rule for the gardener should be that he will

have only one of these flowering at a time if he is saving the seed. Similarly he can expect trouble if one of these is flowering at the same time in a neighbor's garden within 100 yards of his. Crossing can be expected, too, if two varieties of cabbages are raised within 100 yards of each other.

The flowers are pollinated chiefly by bees. As a rule bees will not go from one type of plant to another while collecting honey, preferring to collect from one source, such as apple blossoms or goldenrod, at one time. But in the case of the brassicas, the cabbage family, the bees do not differentiate between broccoli and cabbage, or any of the others, and will gather from all at the same time.

Commercial growers strive for much more than 100 yards between varieties or the various members of this family, with one mile given as the minimum distance. Such a distance is impractical for most home gardeners to consider.

2. *Biennials*. The second problem area with growing these vegetables for seeds is that all of them except broccoli are biennials, requiring two growing seasons to produce seeds, and thus the plants have to be carried through a winter. This can be difficult, particularly in northern areas, and is most difficult with cauliflower.

**CABBAGE** (*Brassica oleracea capitata*). Biennial. Perfect flowers, having both male and female parts. Pollinated by bees. May be self-sterile.

Cabbages grown for seed have the usual head the first year, and in the second, produce a seed stem with branches. The stem may grow as high as five feet, and should be staked for support. Leaves, much smaller than first-year cabbage leaves, and bright yellow flowers grow on the stem and the many branches. Pods develop containing up to twenty seeds each. When the pods turn yellow, the seeds are mature. While an

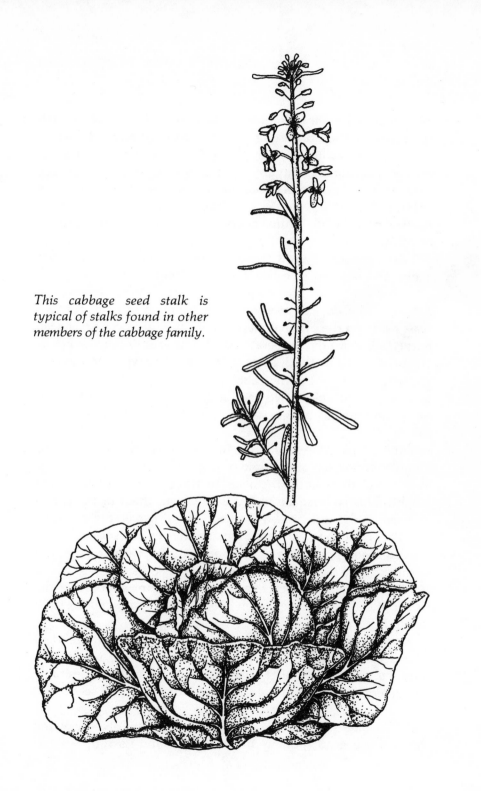

*This cabbage seed stalk is typical of stalks found in other members of the cabbage family.*

individual plant may produce as much as a half-pound of seed, the gardener should raise at least six cabbage plants for seed. Some of the plants may be self-sterile, so a quantity of seeds can be guaranteed only by raising several plants. Cabbage requires a cool period between the two growing seasons to force bolting. The period, studies have shown, can range from about thirty days at temperatures below 50° F. to sixty days at 60° F. or below.

Two methods of growing seed crops are practiced commercially, and can be used by the home gardener.

1. *The seed-to-seed method.* Plants remain in place for two seasons, from the original planting until the seed crop has been harvested. If winter temperatures in your area seldom go below 10° F., try this method, since it involves less work and avoids the trouble of storing the cabbages through the winter. Plants can be spaced about two feet apart in rows four feet apart, with the small cabbage varieties planted more closely than this.

Time the planting so that the head of the cabbage will not be completely formed at the time of the heavy frosts. At that time shovel soil up around them up to three-fourths of the plant height. This soil can be pulled away from them in the spring as soon as the soil can be worked. The uncovered plants will be hardy enough to withstand frosts and even late snows.

A common practice is to slash an inch-deep X across the top of the head, to hasten the emergence of the seedstalk.

When this stalk appears, a stake capable of supporting the five-foot stalk should be driven in beside the plant, and the stalk tied to it.

A weakness of this system is that the gardener will tend to raise seed from all the cabbages that survive the winter. He must be particularly alert to rogue out any with undesirable characteristics, to avoid a gradual deterioration of his seed.

2. *The plant-to-seed method.* This method involves growing the cabbage head, pulling and storing it and its root system,

then replanting it in the spring. The gardener will plant cabbages for seed somewhat later than those he will harvest for eating. His aim will be to have the head reach maturity in the late fall, after the first fall frosts, so that it will store well.

For more than enough seed for several years, the gardener might raise eighteen cabbages the first year. This will give him an opportunity to save the twelve best for planting the following year (and of course saving the others for eating). With any luck he will winter over enough so that he can select the six best for planting for seed.

When roguing out undesirable plants, remember that the job must be completed before the first blossoms appear on the second-year plants, or pollen from those undesirable plants may fertilize the plants that are being saved.

Try to store your seed cabbages:

1. Where temperatures will remain as close to 32° F. as possible. This keeps the plant dormant.
2. Where humidity is high, so the plant does not dry out.
3. On shelves, packed closely together, but not piled up.

They should be inspected occasionally during the winter, and any that are rotten should be thrown away.

An ideal storage place is a cold cellar such as is used for storing root crops. Sometimes cabbages are stored in pits and covered with soil. This method provides adequate moisture, and the cabbages will not be harmed if frozen. But there is a greater chance of spoilage going undetected and spreading.

The bulky outer leaves of the cabbage can be removed before storing.

In the spring, as early as the soil can be worked, the cabbage and its root system should be replanted, about two feet apart in rows four feet apart. The cabbage head should be resting on the ground, and thus is several inches lower than it was in its original position.

Cut an inch-deep X in the top of each head, and, when the stalk appears, support it with a stake.

At harvesting time, you'll find the cabbages most uncoopera-
tive. All the seeds do not mature at the same time, so cannot
be harvested easily. The seeds are in small pods, and the first

*Selecting one of the best cabbages for seed production.*

pods will be turning yellow, then brown, and then dehiscing (or splitting open and spilling out their seeds), before the last ones have matured. Cut the plants when the pods begin to change color. Dry them in some way so that any seeds falling from shattered pods can be caught. Piling the plants on a large sheet is one way to do this. The immature pods will ripen and turn in color during this drying period. Strip the pods from the branches, place them in a bag or pillowcase, and beat them with your hands.

If many seeds have been grown, the easiest method to clean the trash from the seeds is to build a screen that will permit these small, round seeds to fall through, but will hold back the trash. Another system, if only a few seeds are grown, is to place the seeds and trash on a slightly inclined plane, such as a table propped up on one side, then work the mass over with your hands, permitting the seeds to roll down and into a container.

The seeds also may be winnowed.

**BROCCOLI** (*Brassica oleracea italica*). Annual. Has perfect flowers, having both male and female parts. Pollination by bees. May be self-sterile.

Broccoli is unlike the other members of this family in that it produces flowers the first year. For this reason it is a good plant for the beginner to try. Broccoli will cross with Brussels sprouts, cabbage, cauliflower, kale, and kohlrabi if any of these are flowering at the same time (mid-summer) as the broccoli flowers, so the gardener should raise but one of these per year for seed. The edible part of broccoli is the mass of buds, which will develop into tiny yellow flowers.

In colder climates, broccoli for seed should be started indoors, in a greenhouse or in a cold frame, with plants set out two weeks before the last expected frost. Set plants eighteen inches apart in rows thirty-six inches apart. Rogue out any weak or off-type plants when setting them out, and again before the plants blossom.

In warmer climates gardeners can sow seeds of the hardy broccoli in the early fall, so that the plants will produce seeds late the following spring.

When most of the seed pods have turned brown and dried, the broccoli plants can be cut. The process of harvesting, threshing and cleaning is the same as for cabbage seed.

**BRUSSELS SPROUTS** (*Brassica oleracea gemmifera*). Biennial. Perfect flowers, having male and female parts. Some may be self-sterile. Pollination by bees. See cabbage for problems with crossing.

Nearly all of the directions for cabbage apply to Brussels sprouts. The grower in the North may have difficulty in carrying the plants through the winter because of the tendency of the small cabbage-like sprouts to dry out in storage. The growing of these seeds is much easier in the more temperate climates, since the plants are very hardy, and thus will survive in the garden, without being uprooted and stored. It is not necessary to slash the tops of the small Brussels sprouts heads to promote growth, as is done with the cabbage heads.

**CAULIFLOWER** (*Brassica oleracea botrytis*). Biennial. Perfect flowers, having male and female parts. For crossing dangers, see cabbage. Pollination by bees.

Most gardeners consider the cauliflower the fussiest of the cabbage family to grow, and the most difficult to raise for seeds. The beginning seed-grower will make the growing of cauliflower seeds one of his later attempts, particularly if he lives in the North. The problem is to carry the parent plant from one growing season to the next.

I proved to my own satisfaction that in northern Vermont it is impossible to carry the cauliflower over either by mulching it in the garden or by storing it in a root cellar. Both attempts were made during one winter; both were dismal failures.

More success can be achieved by starting the seeds in early September in flats, placed in a cold frame. They are repotted into peat pots about six weeks later, and moved into a cool greenhouse. There they are repotted into larger pots in mid-winter, and finally moved into the garden in late April, where they move from the curd (ready to eat) stage to formation of seedstalks.

In warmer climates, such as in California, the seeds are sown in mid-summer, and grown on the seed-to-seed plan.

In either case, the spacing should be ample, since the seed stalk, while smaller than the cabbage, requires more room than the first-year plant. Three feet in each direction is a minimum separation distance for most cauliflower varieties.

Like the other brassicas, the cauliflower produces a seedstalk on which yellow flowers are formed. The seed pods form in the summer, and in the fall turn yellow, and then brown. Like cabbage plants, they can be cut, then piled on a sheet to dry further. Follow the directions under cabbage for harvesting and threshing.

**CHINESE CABBAGE** (*Brassica pekinensis*). Annual. Flowers are perfect, with male and female parts. Pollinated by bees. Self-sterility should be expected.

You might expect this vegetable would cross with cabbage and others in that family we have discussed. But it won't. Instead it will cross with other varieties of Chinese cabbage, as well as with turnips, radishes, rutabagas, and mustard, both cultivated and wild. Professional growers use a quarter-mile as a minimum isolation distance. The home gardener will grow only one from

*Chinese cabbage, labeled to be saved.*

this group in a season for seed, but can grow all of them as crops for eating. Thus only one will be flowering.

Because this is an annual, the crops are sown where the seeds will be produced. The gardener can space plants twelve to sixteen inches apart in rows thirty inches apart.

Gardeners in the North plant Chinese cabbage late, knowing that if it is planted early or if it is transplanted, it may bolt before forming heads. While this may seem desirable for seed production, it means the cabbage is not heading and therefore the chance is lost to cull out plants with undesirable characteristics such as loose heads.

The northern gardener has three possible methods of growing this vegetable for seed.

1. As just described, plant early, knowing the plants will produce seed without producing a head. This assures you of

seed, but makes it impossible to rogue to get the best possible heads.

2. Plant as late as mid-June, and thus have the opportunity to rogue out undesirable plants. You will be taking a chance on getting mature seeds before the first heavy frost.

3. Plant in the late summer, mulch the plants after the first heavy frosts, and hope that heavy snows will also protect this hardy plant. In the spring, rogue out any undesirable plants as they head.

In mild areas, seed sown in the fall will head, then produce seed stalks and yellow flowers the following spring.

The Chinese cabbage seed stalk is not as large as the cabbage stalk. The seed is found in small pods, and harvesting is the same as for cabbage seed.

**KALE** (*Brassica oleracea acephala*). Biennial. Flowers are perfect, having male and female parts. Pollinated by bees. May be self-sterile.

Hardiest of the brassicas, kale can be grown even in the north by the seed-to-seed method. Plant as for a food crop, either in early spring or following some other crop in mid-summer. In the far north, a mulch applied after the first heavy frosts will give the plants added protection. Plants will produce seed stalks, blossoms and small seed pods the following summer and fall. Stake up the stalks. For harvesting directions, follow those for Cabbage.

Remember that kale is a member of the Brassica oleracea group, and will cross with all other members of that group. See *Cabbage*.

*Kale, one of the hardiest of the vegetables.*

Because kale is so hardy, it is an excellent choice for the person who wishes to try to raise the seeds of one of the brassica family.

**KOHLRABI** (*Brassica oleracea caulorapa*). Biennial. Has perfect flowers, with male and female parts. Pollinated by bees. May be self-sterile.

Kohlrabi, one of the most curious of the cabbage family, is grown for its ball-like swollen stem.

In more temperate areas, seed is planted in the fall. The following spring, the crop is carefully inspected, with any plants having other than uniform stems of the desired color being rogued out.

In more northern areas, gardeners may choose between mulching the plants after the first heavy frosts, then uncovering them in the spring, or pulling up the plants, roots and all, in the late fall, storing them, following the directions for cabbage, then replanting them in the spring. If either of these methods

*Swollen stem is the part of kohlrabi that is eaten.*

is used, seeding should be timed so that growth is halted by heavy frosts before the plant has reached full maturity.

Since the plant produces an ungainly seed stalk the second year, the home gardener should give his plants ample room, perhaps twenty-four inches apart in rows thirty inches apart. Harvesting and storage are the same as for cabbage.

# CRUCIFERAE

## Root Crops

All of these root crops grow best in cool, moist climates. The group that will cross includes turnip, radish, rape, mustard, rutabaga, Chinese cabbage, as well as wild varieties of mustard and turnip. The home gardener raising seed should permit only one of these to flower at any one time in his garden, and he should cut back any wild varieties to avoid crosses between them and his vegetable crop. Professional growers set a quarter-mile as the minimum isolation distance.

**TURNIP** (*Brassica rapa*). Biennial. Pollinated by bees. Perfect flowers, having both male and female parts.

This hardy plant is relatively easy to grow for seeds, so is a good one for the beginner to try if he wants to attempt to grow seed from one of the biennial brassicas.

The turnip can be grown by two methods when raising seeds:

1. *Root-to-seed*. This method must be used only in the most northern areas of the country, and involves digging and storing the roots. An advantage of this method is that it permits inspection of the roots, so that those that do not store well, or are not uniform in size, shape, or color can be discarded.

The home gardener using this method will plant for seed much later than for a crop for eating. Planting is timed so that the crop will barely reach maturity in late fall. The roots are dug at that time or in early winter. The tops are cut back to one inch from the crowns, then the roots are placed in damp sand and stored in a near-freezing site, such as a root cellar. (If you have a tried and true method for storing carrots, for eating during the winter, use it for turnips.)

In the spring, as early as the ground can be worked, set the roots out, with crowns at ground level, eighteen inches apart in rows two feet apart.

2. *Seed-to-seed*. This method can be used throughout most of the country, and even in cold areas if snows are heavy enough to protect the roots during the winter. While rouging, to discard roots that are not uniform in shape, size, or color, is not possible using this method, it is much less work.

The first year's crop can be planted, then thinned to three or four inches apart, in rows two feet apart. Planting time

*Turnips, ready to be transplanted for seed production.*

must be figured for each geographical area. The gardener should aim for roots that have not quite reached market size when cold weather halts the growth. This means mid-summer planting in northern regions and early fall planting further south. Prior to the second year, enough turnips should be harvested to provide eighteen inches of space between plants.

The seed stalks the second year should be watched carefully, and, when the seed pods have turned yellow, the stalk should be cut, then can be handled like cabbage stalks.

**RUTABAGA** (*Brassica napus napobrassica*). Biennial. Pollinated by bees. Perfect flowers, having both male and female parts.

This vegetable is also commonly known as the *Swede turnip*, and is much like the turnip, except that it is most commonly grown in the northern part of this country, and in the cooler areas of Canada, while turnip is commonly grown further south. Colors range from white to the most common buff to green and purple.

*Rutabaga in its first year of growth.*

For growing instructions, see instructions for turnips. The only major difference is that rutabaga must be planted earlier than turnip, since it is slower growing. For the seed-to-seed method, sow in early August; for root-to-seed, plant in early June.

## HORSE-RADISH (*Amoracia rusticana*). Perennial.

Horse-radish is propagated by planting sections of either the main root or the smaller lateral roots of a parent plant. Those planting it should be certain they want horse-radish growing in that site henceforth, since, once established, horse-radish is very difficult to eliminate. Any root left behind in digging will grow again.

In the late fall or early winter, when the root is at its pungent best, dig up root, cut into sections four to six inches long, and replant, a foot apart, with the large ends up, as they were growing.

**RADISH** (*Raphanus sativus*). Annual. (But the larger Oriental or winter radishes are biennial.) Cross-pollinated by bees. Perfect flowers.

The annual radish is that spicy vegetable of which we grow too many in our frantic desire for something quick and in quantity from the garden in the early spring. It will cross easily with other radish varieties, and with others in its group, as explained at the beginning of this section, and so only one variety of the group should be permitted to flower at the same time in the home garden. For professional growers, the minimum isolation distance is a quarter-mile.

If the beginner has difficulty getting seeds from radish plants he should consider these three possible reasons:

1. Bees are required for pollination, and often the small white-to-lilac flower of the radish will not attract bees, if other flowers are available to them.

2. Hot weather. The best-tasting radishes are grown in the cool of the spring. The best crops of seeds are grown in cool weather, with production cut when periods of temperatures over 90° F. are experienced.

3. Dry weather, too, results in fewer radish seeds, although the radish is more tolerant of dry weather than are the cabbage and its near-relatives.

Two methods are used in growing radish seeds:

1. *Root-to-seed*. Plant seeds as for growing for the table, thinning them to two inches apart in rows as close as a foot apart. In three or four weeks, depending on the variety of root, the radishes will be large enough to eat. Rogue them, saving the radishes that have the best size, shape, and color, and eating

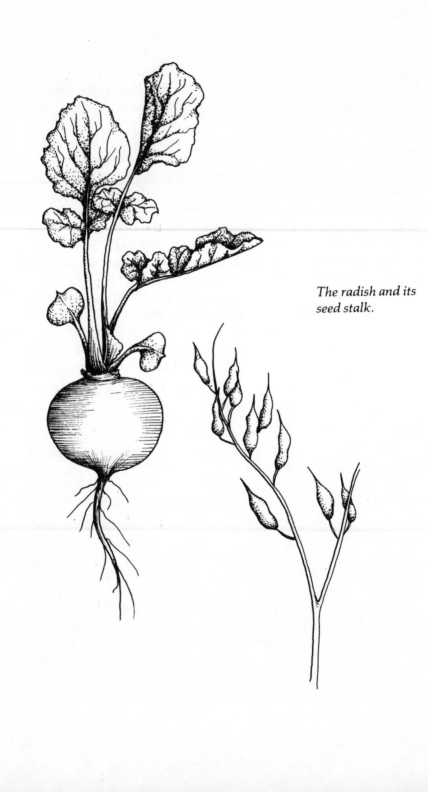

*The radish and its
seed stalk.*

the remainder. Prepare the roots for planting by cutting off all but about one inch of the leaves. Look closely at the top of a radish. You will see small central leaves beginning to develop. Do not cut these.

When replanting, set the roots in the soil so that the crown of the radish is at ground level. They will produce seed stalks two to three feet tall, so give them enough room—about eight inches apart in rows three feet apart.

The careful gardener will rogue once more, pulling up and discarding those plants that bolt first, since early bolting is not a characteristic to encourage. Careful roguing at this time and earlier will do much to maintain the quality of the seed grown.

2. *Seed-to-seed*. This method saves time and labor, but results in poorer seed, since roguing out the undesirable plants is not as selective as with the first method.

Plant seeds in rows three feet apart, and thin plants to eight or more inches apart. When thinning, rogue out undesirable

*A row of white radishes being thinned.*

plants. A better job of roguing can be done if the gardener pulls away enough soil from the top of the roots so that he can see their color. Any that are off-colored should be removed.

In the north, planting in the spring is advised. Further south, the gardener may plant in the fall, and plan on getting a seed stalk growth the following spring.

The radish seeds develop in pods. Unlike the cabbage seed pods, these pods will not break open when dry, thus the precautions for saving seeds from pods that break open need not be taken.

Plants should remain in the garden until most of the pods are brown. Home gardeners can open the pods by hand. Dry them further if they are difficult to open. The seeds are yellow at first, even when mature, but will gradually turn to the brown familiar to most gardeners.

The biennial radish, called *daikon* by the Japanese, is unfamiliar to many gardeners who would appreciate both its taste and the ease with which it can be stored to be cooked in the winter. To raise these for seed, follow instructions for turnip.

# LEGUMINOSAE

## Pea Family

Beginners, here's the starting place if you're interested in growing seeds.

It's hard to go wrong growing peas or beans for seed. You don't need to provide the walled security and isolation of a nunnery in order to defend and preserve their purity. A row of some other crop—preferably a tall one—between rows of different varieties of peas, and 150 feet between varieties of beans will prevent crosses.

They are annuals, so growing plants need not be carried from one season to another. And the seeds are large. Harvesting them is easy.

There's another plus to raising them. If you are careful (and lucky), and industrious enough to mind your peas and beans (and still lucky), you can produce a superior variety of either one. You will have vegetables that do best in your garden, because over several generations they have become acclimated to your soil and growing conditions.

You'll be tempted to grow your usual crops of these two vegetables, and then, when you have picked what you want to eat, let the remainder dry on the vines, and save them for seeds.

Don't do it. You may be saving from less than desirable plants, and you probably will be saving late-growing seeds, and thus possibly breeding that characteristic into your seeds.

There are many ways to divide your rows between eating and saving for seeds. A recommended way is to mark off ten or fifteen feet of a row for seeds. Put a string around that section. It will remind you and others not to pick from it. Treat this section like royalty. Give it that extra amount of compost. (But not too much fertilizer that's heavy on nitrogen. That will produce lush plants, and fewer seeds.) Carefully rogue out any weak or undesirable plants. Make certain the individual plants have elbow room enough to attain full growth. Weed that plot so the crop does not compete with other plants for food, light, or moisture.

And, when you have grown, harvested, dried, and packaged your seed, mark the container carefully with the year of growth, and the variety of seeds. Some years ago I planted green beans, and carefully saved a section of a row for seeds. The beans were delicious and the bushes were loaded with them. I'd made a good choice. Suddenly I realized—I'd forgotten what variety I had planted. Now each fall, after I have dried and packaged some of those beans for seeds, I mark the container, "Brand X." It's a reminder to me not to make that particular mistake again.

**PEA** (*Pisum sativum*). Annual. Self-fertile, but to preserve purity of seed, avoid planting adjacent rows of different varieties.

If you can grow a good crop of peas for eating, you can grow them for seeds. Peas do best when planted before the final spring frost, and ideal growing conditions for them are slowly warming days. Peas are planted early—in December and January in the Coastal Plains, Gulf Coast regions, and California; in late January and February in the mid-South, and April and early May in the northernmost areas of the country. Pea plants are hardy enough to live through frosts, although heavy freezing will delay the crop. The gardener who gets the earliest crop of peas gets the best peas, and this is true equally of peas for seed.

During the growing season rogue out any weak plants, or plants that are off-color or undesirable in any other way. Plants with small, narrow leaves are commonly found among some varieties, and should be rouged out.

When the peas reach edible size, resist the temptation to harvest them for eating. Wait another month. By now the pods are brown and dry, and the peas inside them are dry enough to rattle when the pods are shaken.

Many commercial growers pull up the plants, then stack or windrow them for further drying. If you have the time, try this method: Pick the pods by pulling up the plants, then stripping off all of the pods. Spread them out under cover, such as in a barn, for further drying. By doing this you will avoid the possibility of the pods getting rained on, and the damp peas sprouting and becoming worthless as seeds. If well dried, they can be left in the pods for weeks or months. Removing them from the pods is a good job for winter, when there isn't as much work to do. You should get at least a pound of seed per twelve feet of row.

There are several methods of removing the seed from the pods. If you harvest one bushel or less, the seeds may be removed by hand. Because the pods are dry, this job can be done quickly.

If you have more than a bushel, try threshing them out. Spread

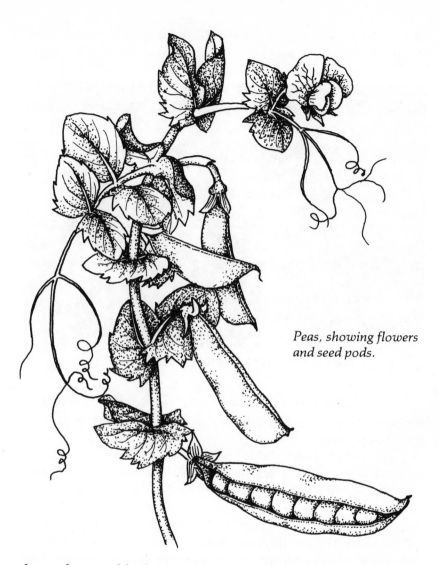

*Peas, showing flowers
and seed pods.*

the pods on a blanket or canvas, and beat them with a flail
made of two sticks attached by a short piece of leather. Control
your enthusiasm as you thresh. Break open the pods, but don't
break apart the peas.

Since the peas tend to fall to the blanket or canvas surface,
most of the trash can be removed quickly with a rake or pitchfork. Then gather the corners of the blanket or canvas to bring
the peas together in a pile, and remove the remainder of the
trash by hand.

*A section of peas, reserved for seed production.*

If dirt and trash remain in the seeds, remove them by taking the seeds outside on a windy day and pouring them from one bowl to another.

If you are in doubt about how dry the seeds are, after three or more weeks of drying, let them dry another week or two, well spread out so that moisture is not held in under layers of seed.

The professional seed grower has moisture computers that will read out the moisture percentage at the touch of a button. The amateur can't afford this equipment, so it is meaningless to quote desired percentages of moisture to him. Remember that seed viability depends on low moisture content as well as low temperature, and that maintenance of either at a low level will do much to extend the viability of the seed. Remember, too, that, no matter how dry the seed is at the time of storing, it will soon have the moisture level of the air around it. Thus the emphasis on finding a cool, dry location for storage.

Many people recommend storing peas and beans in airtight

containers. I don't. Several attempts at this under varying conditions have resulted in peculiar smells, the growth of fungi, spoilage—and lower viability. I have had no difficulty with placing seeds in burlap bags and storing them under cool, dry conditions.

**BEAN** (*Phaseolus vulgaris*). Annual. Perfect flower, containing male and female parts. Usually self-pollinating before flower opens, so there is little chance of cross-pollination.

While beans cross-pollinate more than peas, there is still little opportunity for this, so a row of some vegetable between rows of different varieties of beans will decrease even the minimum opportunity for cross-pollinating. For greatest protection, plant varieties 150 feet apart.

All of the beans are grown for seed in the same manner. And all, to some degree, have the same limiting factor when being raised for seed. They must be started after all danger of frost is past, and they must be harvested before freezing injures the seed. Thus many areas of the North simply do not have a long enough growing season for some varieties of beans.

An example is the lima bean. Burpee's famed *Best*, a pole lima bean, requires 92 days to reach eating size. Add another six weeks to this for maturity as seeds, and that's a requirement for a 134-day growing season between even light frosts—far too much for most of the northern states.

If you have grown such dry beans as navy or kidney beans with success, you can, of course, grow these as well as snap beans for seed without worrying about the length of the growing season.

When growing these beans for seed, grow them as you would for a crop for eating, but rogue out any plants with undesirable qualities. Beans are planted after the danger of frost is past, and will react to weather in other ways. They will

Beans are an ideal crop for the
person who wishes to try saving
seeds.

drop blossoms during a heat wave, and fail to produce if the weather turns cool and raining.

Plant bush beans in rows two feet apart, with plants thinned to four inches apart. Pole bean rows should be at least three feet apart.

The harvesting time as seeds can be estimated by watching the crop reach the harvesting size for eating, with the pods nearly full grown and the beans not fully developed. The beans should be ready for harvesting as seeds about six weeks later, or when most of the pods have turned brown.

The person who is harvesting only one or two bushels may find it easy to pick the beans, spread them out (indoors if you have rainy autumns) to cure for a week or two, then shell them.

For larger amounts, pull up the plants, let them dry in piles or windrows for one or two weeks, until brittle, then flail them. If rain can be expected during the drying period, try to dry them indoors.

In flailing, most of the trash can be removed with a pitchfork or rake, with the remainder removed by winnowing.

Seeds should be stored in a cool, dry place—not in airtight containers.


**LIMA BEAN** (*Phaseolus lunatus*) can't be grown for eating in the green stage in many of the northern regions. Ideally they should have two months of above 50° F. night temperatures, with planting delayed until the soil is warm. Add six more weeks of frost-free weather at the end of this two-month period for growing these beans for seed, and the reason they can't be grown in the north for seed is obvious.

Bush and pole varieties are available. All the steps of growing, harvesting, drying and storage are the same as for other beans. They can be damaged during and after harvesting, so care should be taken with them.

*Lima beans, not yet ready to be picked for seeds.*

**COWPEA** (*Vigna sinensis*) is grown in the South (where it is often called a *southern pea* or a *field pea*: the green pea of the rest of the nation is an *English pea*) and in California (where it is called a *black-eyed bean*). Many families in the South save this seed each year, proud of the taste qualities of the strain they nurture.

This warm-weather crop is grown much like lima beans, with planting delayed until the soil is warm, when seed is planted three inches apart, in rows thirty to thirty-six inches apart.

Follow instructions for beans in harvesting, drying, and storage.

**SOYBEAN** (*Glycine max*). This is a crop of growing interest to the home gardener, because of the many uses and the high protein content of the soybean, with the larger-seeded garden varieties the choice to grow.

Like lima beans, most of the soybeans can be planted only when the soil is warm, and most have a long growing season. However, several seed companies in northern areas have worked on, and now offer for sale, soybeans with growing seasons short enough to be grown in most areas of the United States.

Follow instructions for beans for harvesting, drying, and storing.


# *MALVACEAE*

## Mallow Family

This family includes familiar flowers, such as the hollyhock, an important commercial plant, cotton, a few trees, weeds—and one garden vegetable, okra.


**OKRA** (*Hibiscus esculentus*). Annual. Self-pollinating.

This plant produces a yellow flower with a red center followed within several days by a pod which is harvested for eating before it has become fully developed.

For seeds, pods should be left on plants to become woody, and with the seeds fully developed. Harvest pods in late fall, crack them open, and remove the seed. Because this plant is self-pollinating, there is no reason to isolate the crop raised for seed.

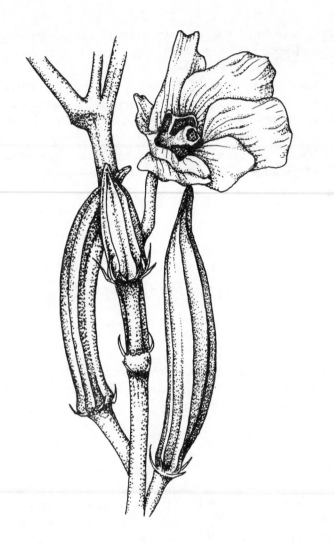

*Okra, its flower and pods.*

# UMBELLIFERAE

## Parsley Family

The gardener who wishes to grow seeds of biennials is encouraged to select from this group. Carrying the plants over to the second year of growth is not a major problem with these, as it can be, for example, with the members of the cabbage group. The major problem for home growers is that the various varieties of each will cross unless separated by long distances, and the carrot will cross with the weed Queen Anne's lace, which is an annual.

Most of the seeds in this family have low viability, so should be tested before planting. All of them flower and form seed the second year.

**CARROT** (*Daucus carota sativa*). Biennial. Perfect flowers, with both male and female parts. Pollinated by insects.

There are two methods of growing seed:

1. *Root-to-seed*, the recommended method. Plant late enough in spring so that the plant reaches maturity in late fall. This plant can be dug up any time before the ground freezes. The tops should be cut off, with care being taken not to cut into the growing point of the plant's crown. Leave an inch of growth.

Rogue out the crop at this time, reserving for table use any carrots that are misshapen, off-color, small, cracked, or damaged while being harvested.

In mild climates, the carrot can be replanted immediately after this roguing. In cooler areas, replanting in the late fall is possible, too, with a heavy mulch giving the roots more than

*Carrot and its second-year stalk.*

adequate protection. Or the roots can be stored for spring planting.

Near-freezing temperatures and high humidity are ideal for storage. These conditions will be found in a storage cellar. For further protection, carrots can be stored in boxes of damp sand or sawdust.

In the spring, when the soil can be worked, the stored carrots should be checked over, and any that have shriveled or decayed should be discarded. They should not be left to dry out before replanting, but should be set out quickly in moist soil. If the soil tends to be dry, soak each carrot after it is planted. Set them out one foot apart, in rows three feet apart, with the carrot's crown set at or just below soil surface level.

There are two common methods for setting them out.

One is to insert a shovel into the soil, then push it forward, and plant a carrot in the space. Make certain that the soil is firm up around each carrot as it is planted.

The second is to rototill the soil, then simply press the carrot down into the loosened soil, making certain the root is planted deep enough so that the crown is at soil surface level when the soil has been packed around it.

2. *Seed-to-seed* is the second method of growing carrots for seed. This method involves leaving the carrot in place for two seasons. This involves less work, but has disadvantages. The grower cannot rouge out undesirable roots, so the quality of seeds may deteriorate gradually. Carrying carrots through the winter, too, can be troublesome. Alternate freezing and thawing may thrust the roots up out of the ground, (a problem that usually can be avoided by mulching them). Finally, the gardener may tend to crowd his crop using this method, leaving too many carrots in the row the first growing season, and not reducing the number of carrots to space plants one foot apart in rows three feet apart the second year of growth.

No matter which method is used, the soil should be loose and high in organic matter, and never should be permitted to dry out. Weeds should be eliminated to provide ideal growing conditions.

Commercial growers separate varieties by a minimum of one mile. Your alternative must be to carry but one variety into the second year growth, although other varieties of course can be grown for first-year harvesting. Check your area for Queen Anne's lace, and make certain it is cut back and not blossoming when your carrots blossom the second year.

If you've grown carrots only as annuals for eating, you'll be surprised at that second year of growth—two to six feet high, with a fairly large head, and a series of branches beneath it. Flowers will appear first on the head, then the top and finally the lower branches. This is also the order of development of

*Queen Anne's lace looks much like the second-year growth of carrots.*

*Carrots being harvested for storage.*

seeds. The seeds are ready for harvesting when the heads of the top branches have turned brown. This will be in September in most areas. They will not shatter easily, so exact timing of harvesting isn't necessary.

For harvesting a small crop, pull up the entire plant, and form small piles of them. They should be cured until the stalks will snap when bent. This may take two or three weeks in moist climates. It can be speeded up by placing the plants under cover to cure.

Another method of harvesting is to cut off the heads as they mature (turn brown), and take them indoors to dry.

Rub the seed heads together to free the seed. This will produce the seeds, plus stems and other unwanted material. The quickest way to remove the latter is to build a screen that will permit the seeds to fall through but will sort out the other debris.

The seeds you thus retrieve will have small spines. Commercial growers remove these so that the seed can be used in mechanical seeders. If you wish to remove them, rub the seeds briskly between your hands.

**CELERIAC** (*Apium graveolens rapaceum*). Biennial. Perfect flowers, having both male and female parts. Cross-pollinated by insects.

This vegetable, unfamiliar to many gardeners, is grown for its roots. While it is closely related to celery, the methods used to grow seed are very similar to those for carrots.

Celery and celeriac will cross, so only one of these should be growing the second year for seed in any season.

In the second year, the plants should be watched carefully, since all of the seeds will not mature at the same time, and the seed tends to shatter. You can save this early seed by holding the browned heads in a paper bag and shaking them.

Follow instructions for carrots for growing, harvesting, and drying the seeds.

**CELERY** (*Apium graveolens dulce*). Biennial. Perfect flowers, with both male and female parts. Cross-pollinated by insects.

This is probably the most difficult of the plants in this family to raise for seed, because of the greater difficulty in wintering the plants.

In the North, because of celery's long growing season, this vegetable must be started indoors or in a cold frame, then transplanted outdoors. This is not necessary in the areas of milder weather that provide the 115–135 days of a growing season this crop requires.

In the fall, select the best plants for seed. They should be dug up, roots intact, then placed in a cold cellar, with the roots in soil, and the vegetation blanketed in straw. Near-freezing temperatures and high humidity are required.

After the danger of frost is past in the spring, uncover the plants, remove the rotted leaves and stalks, and replant, two feet apart in rows three feet apart.

In warm areas such as California and the South, the timing is changed by sowing in July, then transplanting the plants in January. This avoids the need to store the plants.

The second-year growth is two to three feet tall and extremely bushy. The tiny white flowers appear first on the top of the plant, then bloom on the lower branches. Seeds will turn brown and be ready for harvesting in this same order. Since many seeds can be lost through shattering, you should try to save the earlier seeds by shaking the top heads into a paper bag.

Follow directions for harvesting given for carrots. Dry heads on a canvas, so seeds that fall will not be lost.

Remember that celery and celeriac will cross, so in any one season, you will have only one of these blossoming.

**PARSLEY** (*Petroselinum crispum*). Biennial. Has perfect flowers, with male and female parts. Pollinated by insects.

Parsley seeds, even under ideal conditions, do not retain their viability for more than one to two years. New seed should be harvested each year.

Parsley seeds, slow to germinate, may be speeded along by soaking them overnight the night before planting. They can be started indoors or in cold frames, then transplanted to one foot apart.

In the fall, select the most desirable plants, and transplant them to where you wish them to grow by digging them up with a spadeful of soil. Set them two feet apart in rows two feet apart. After the first few heavy frosts, cover them with a mulch of leaves or hay. They will survive well, even in northern areas.

Uncover them as growth starts in the spring. They will grow to two or more feet in height, with many branches and small flower heads. Seeds are ready for harvesting when they turn brown, in September in most areas, and will shatter. The first seeds can be collected by shaking the heads in a paper bag.

When most of the heads have turned brown, cut them, and let them cure indoors, on canvas or papers so any seeds that fall will not be lost.

Handle as carrot seeds (but these do not have spines).


**PARSNIP** (*Pastinaca sativa*). Biennial. Perfect flowers, having male and female parts. Pollinated by insects.

Parsnip seeds lose viability in one or two years, so fresh seed should be grown each year. This is the slowest-growing member of this family.

Parsnips can be grown either seed-to-seed or root-to-seed, as explained under carrots. You will be tempted to use the former method, because even in the coldest climates, parsnips will winter over without difficulty.

For superior seed, you will use the root-to-seed method, digging up the parsnips in the early spring, when they are ordinarily dug up for eating, then replanting them three feet apart in rows three feet apart, with the crowns at soil level. For the best seed, select the best of the roots for replanting, and dine on the remainder. You can, of course, dig the roots in the fall, store them as you would carrots, then replant them in the spring.

The second year the plant will send up a bushy seed stalk three to four feet in height. The yellowish flowers are followed by the brown seeds in the fall. Harvest as for carrots. Since parsnip seeds shatter, shake the early heads into a paper bag to avoid loss.

# SOLANACEAE

## Nightshade Family

This family includes the eggplant, pepper, potato, and tomato. Most growers of seed will want to try one of these, probably the tomato. Once more—don't try to save seed from the hybrid varieties. It won't work. (And if you *do* try it, as you will if you are the curious type, expect some seed that won't germinate, plus plants that lack the uniformity and vigor of their parents, and even do not resemble them, since the tendency is for them to revert to the type of plants used to create the hybrid.)

For each of these vegetables there are open-pollinated varieties with admirable qualities, and seeds that will not give you unpleasant surprises.

**EGGPLANT** (*Solanum melongena*). Annual. Perfect flowers, with male and female parts. Self-pollinated, but crossing will occur, since flowers sometimes attract insects.

Eggplant likes a growing season that is both long and warm. However, by starting plants indoors or in cold frames, and setting them out when the soil has warmed up, gardeners in all but the coldest parts of the country can raise eggplants.

While cross-pollination is not a major problem, you will avoid any possibility of this if you raise only one variety during a season when you expect to save seed.

Identify and save for seed the best fruits on several of your best plants. The remaining plants can produce for eating, after any with undesirable traits have been rouged out.

If possible, leave the fruit on the plant until it falls off, an indication that the seeds are mature. If frosts threaten, and the

*The eggplant, its blossom and its fruit.*

fruit is ripe enough for eating, pick it and take it indoors. In about two weeks (don't wait until it is rotting) the fruit will produce mature seeds.

Cut the fruit and remove the placenta, or the seed-bearing portion. Place this in a container (a glass bowl works fine), add water, and work the mass with the fingers. Gradually the seeds will separate and sink to the bottom, and the remaining material and water can be poured off. Several washings may be necessary.

Spread the seeds on paper towels or screens, and dry them thoroughly. If, after drying, the seeds are stuck together, rub them together gently in your hands to separate them.

*Here's an eggplant selected for seed production.*

**PEPPER** (*Capsicum annuum*). Annual, but perennial in tropical areas. Perfect flowers, with male and female parts. Self-pollinating, but some crossing can be expected if different varieties are planted in adjacent rows, due to bee action.

Grow plants in usual way. Rogue out any undesirable plants, to avoid cross-pollination with better plants. Select and identify excellent fruits on several of your best plants. Let these ripen far beyond stage where you would ordinarily pick them for eating. They are ready for seed production when they have turned color and have begun to shrivel. If your growing season

*Hundreds of seeds are tucked into a single pepper.*

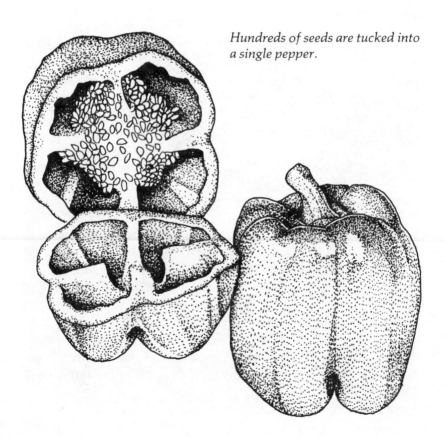

does not permit them to ripen that far, pick peppers and take them indoors to ripen further.

Cut open pepper and remove seed. If this is done carefully, there will be little or no unwanted material mixed with the seeds. Dry thoroughly and store.

**TOMATO** (*Lycopersicon esculentum*). Annual, although it's a perennial in its native South America. Perfect flowers, with male and female parts. Self-pollinated, although some crossing may occur from bee action.

If you have been growing hybrid tomatoes, but would like to grow the open-pollinated varieties for seed as well as for eating, try several varieties the first year. In this way you can most quickly find the variety or varieties that best meet your needs. Plant at least three plants of each variety, separating the varieties by as much garden space as possible.

Tomatoes are tropical plants, and do best in long and hot growing seasons. Those of us in cooler areas know the race we watch each summer, wondering whether the peak of the tomato season will beat the first killing frost. In areas such as this, the seed-grower can strive for early producers.

Identify and mark several of the best and earliest plants of each variety. Let fruit reach full ripeness, then pick the best of them from those plants. Cut them open and scoop out seeds and pulp, mixing seeds and pulp from several plants, but of course keeping the varieties separate. Place mixture in glass jar, with a jar for each variety, and add a small amount of water. Stir two or three times daily. The fermentation that results aids in separation of the seeds from the other materials. Depending on the room temperature, the seeds will separate and sink to the bottom of the jar in from two (warm room) to four days. Add water, pour off pulp, repeating this procedure until seeds are clean.

Spread out on paper towels or screen to dry.

*The perfect flowers and tiny, immature fruit of the tomato plant.*

**POTATO** (*Solanum tuberosum*). Annual. Self-pollinated.

The true seed of the potato is used only in breeding programs. The tuber (that's the potato) is used for propagation as well as for eating. The tubers grown specifically for propagation are often called seed potatoes.

If you want to raise potatoes for both eating and propagation, start with certified disease-free potatoes. Mark the plants that are healthiest and most disease-free, and take your seed potatoes from them. I have tried planting with both the small and the large potatoes from these plants, and see no difference.

*Foliage of a potato plant, and its seedball.*

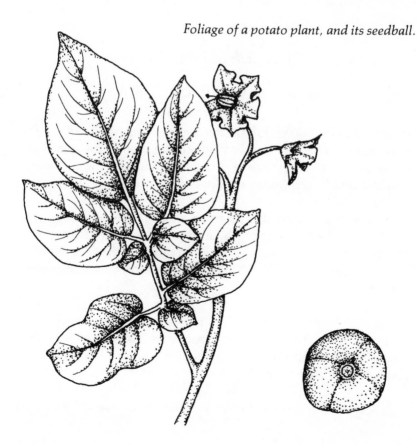

It is logical, then, to eat the larger potatoes and save the smaller ones to start the next season's crop.

Potatoes, of course, have been and are grown from seed. A famous example is that of the Burbank potato, which was one of twenty-three otherwise worthless seedlings grown by Luther Burbank from seed saved from a single potato seedball.

You may not find many seedballs in your patch of highly selected civilized potatoes, but if you do come across a potato plant that bears seed (the seed ball resembles a tiny green tomato), and you want to experiment, save the seed for planting early the next spring. Just don't count on it for your whole crop of potatoes.

# CUCURBITACEAE

## Gourd or Cucumber Family

If you've been successful raising peas or beans for seed, and now want to try your hand at something slightly more complicated, here is your next move. The family includes the cucumber, gourd, squash, pumpkin, muskmelon, (including cantaloupe), and watermelon.

You've probably raised some or all of these for eating. Try one that you're confident with, and raise it for seeds. Remember to follow the rules to avoid unwanted mixes of these vegetables. Here's a case where failures often produce most startling results.

First, a few general rules:

1. Don't worry about crosses between any combinations of cucumbers, squashes, and melons. They won't happen. You won't raise squash-melon, or a melon-cucumber, despite what some old gardener may tell you.

2. Crosses will occur between varieties of each. Thus two

varieties of cucumbers will cross, and this is undesirable if you are saving seed.

  3. But don't worry about it if you are growing crops to eat, not for seed. The female blossom will dominate, so, for example, all of the acorn squash on a single plant will be the same for eating purposes, even though some of the blossoms were pollinated from male acorn squash blossoms, and others from male zucchini squash blossoms.

  Let's start right out with a discussion of squash and pumpkins, since this is where much of the confusion begins for the seed grower. There are just a few simple rules to learn, then you'll feel that superiority that can come when you understand what few others have mastered.

**SQUASH** (*Cucurbita*). Annual. Monoecious, with male and female blossoms on each plant. Cross-pollinated, usually by bees.

  What about crosses between pumpkins and squash? Is there any easy-to-learn rule that just can't be forgotten? Unfortunately, no. They don't divide simply and logically, such as all winter squash in one group, all summer squash in another, and pumpkin in a third.
  Instead there are four species (you may find but three listed in older references), and here are their easily recognized characteristics, and the best-known varieties of each species:

  1. *Cucurbita maxima*. Vines 15–20 feet long. Huge leaves. Stem is soft, round, and hairy. Long growing season. Includes Buttercup, Hubbard, Delicious, and Hokkiado Pumpkin.

  2. *Cucurbita moschata*. Large leaves and spreading vines. The smooth, five-sided corky stem flares out as it joins the fruit. Butternut.

3. *Cucurbita pepo*. Both bush and long-vined. Stem is five-sided. Branches, too, have five sides, and spines. All summer squash. Zucchini, Yellow Crookneck, Vegetable Spaghetti, Acorn, Lady Godiva, White Buch Scallop, Cocozelle, and the common pumpkin.

4. *Cucurbita mixta*. This group formerly was lumped with *Cucurbita moschata*, and has similar characteristics. White Cushaw. Green-striped Cushaw.

The varieties within each species *will* cross. And research has shown that there is also some crossing *between* varieties of different species, specifically:

1. *C. pepo* and *C. moschata*.

2. *C. pepo* and *C. mixta*.

3. *C. moschata* and *C. maxima*.

In your home garden, do not raise more than one variety from each species. In a large planting, a distance of 500 feet is usually enough to prevent crossing. Separate as far as possible varieties of different species if there is some chance of crossing, as indicated in the previous paragraph.

If you wish to raise two or more varieties of a species, or if your over-the-fence neighbor raises them, there is a method you can use to assure the purity of the seed you harvest. It's hand-pollinating.

This involves protection of the female blossom both before and after hand-pollinating, and protection of the male blossom until it has been used for pollinating.

Male and female blossoms from the same plant can be used, since the squashes do not lose vigor if inbred in this way.

Before you begin, you must learn two things: how to tell the male from the female blossom, and how to find buds that will open the following day.

Identifying the male and female blossoms is simple. The

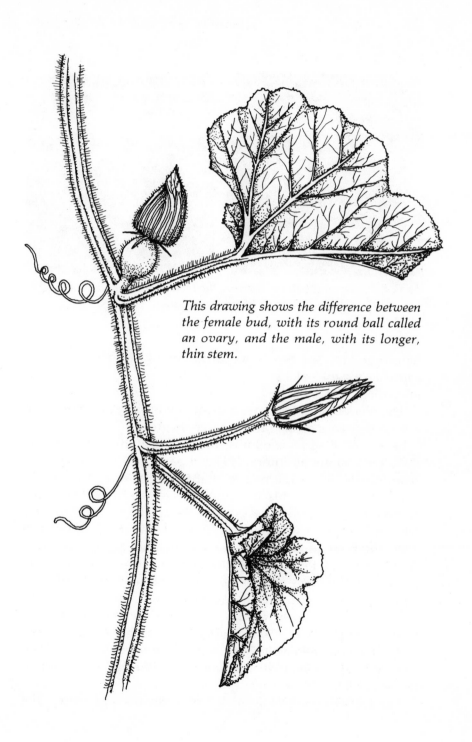

This drawing shows the difference between the female bud, with its round ball called an ovary, and the male, with its longer, thin stem.

*Look for the round ball or ovary at the base of the female bud (left) to differentiate it from the male blossom (right).*

female bud has the beginning of the squash—a miniature fruit called an *ovary*—at its base, while the stem of the male buds leads directly into the bud.

The blossoms that will open the following day are those with a definite orange color, rather than only green.

Select six or so female buds for your first effort, identifying them on a sunny afternoon. Place a paper bag over each one, marking an "F" on the bag so that it will be plain to you the following day that this is one of the female buds. The bags given by supermarkets for pints of ice cream are ideal for this work since they are heavy and thus will endure the dews and even the rains of several days. Tie (but not tightly over the stem), staple (but not through the stem), or paper clip the bag in place, close enough so that no exploring honey bee will find her way into it. Protect an equal number of male buds. The same type bags can be used, or, because the bud needs to be held closed only overnight, simply slip a rubber band over the end of the bud, holding it shut. I tried using twine, and it worked fine, although tying it without damaging the bud was more of a problem.

The following morning, pick one of the male blossoms that

you fastened shut with a rubber band. Carry it to one of the covered female blossoms. Uncover the female blossom, and remove its petals. Take the rubber band off the male blossom and remove its petals. You will see the stamen and its pollen. Gently rub this stamen against the stigma of the female blossom so that the pollen clings to the stigma. Discard the male blossom, and cover the female blossom again with the paper bag. Leave it in place for about four days. Mark the stem of the female blossom in some way so that the right squash can be found at harvesting time. A bright ribbon tied loosely around the stem is one way to do this.

*This fruit is clearly identified for saving.*

Repeat this process for each female blossom. This is one of those simple procedures that can be done much more quickly than it can be described, so don't be talked out of trying it by the detail given here.

The squash and pumpkin plants should be watched during all periods of growth, so that any with undesirable traits can be rogued out.

The seed of the winter varieties and pumpkins is mature when the squash or pumpkin is mature and ready for harvesting, in the fall. The summer squash, however, must grow far beyond the harvesting stage, until it has reached full growth and has hardened. If you have raised zucchini squash, and one hid under the heavy foliage and grew to a huge size, you have grown zucchini to the proper size for seed.

Squash for seed should be harvested in the fall, at about the time of the first frost. Because the squash will keep for many months, there is no urgency about removing the seeds. It's a good job for the early winter. Cut the squash in two, avoiding slicing through the central seed cavity. The seeds and the moist material around them can be removed with a large kitchen spoon. Place all of it in a large bowl, add some water, and work the mixture through your fingers. The seeds will separate gradually. Wash them again, then spread them out on paper or screens to dry. Give them up to a week of drying, moving them about daily so that they do not remain in small, wet piles, retaining the moisture.

These can be kept in a sealed jar. It's a good idea to check them two or three weeks after placing them in the jar. If there is any sign of moisture, spread the seeds out again for further drying. After all the trouble you've gone to, this is not the time to take a chance on spoilage.

And label the container with the variety of seeds and the year of growing. You may remember—and then again you may not.


**PUMPKIN**. All directions for squash apply to pumpkin.

**CUCUMBER** (*Cucumis sativus*). Annual. Monoecius, with separate male and female blossoms. Cross-pollinated by bees.

Cucumbers will not cross with melons or squashes, but will cross with other varieties of cucumbers. The home gardener thus may grow any vegetables in his garden, and still may raise cucumbers for seed, provided he raises only one variety of cucumber. Because bees pollinate the cucumber blossoms, commercial seed growers strive for a distance of at least a mile between varieties. The home gardener should be concerned about any other varieties within a quarter-mile of his, but will probably get an undesired cross only if a neighboring garden is growing a different variety. Some method of cooperation, such as both growing the same variety, can usually be worked out.

The length of the growing season may be a problem for some gardeners in cold climates. Cucumbers for eating may be raised in 60–70 days, with planting started after all danger of frost is past. But the growing season for seeds must be at least five weeks longer to produce the ripe, yellow cucumber that will have the mature seed.

The careful gardener will watch the growth of the cucumber plants through all stages of development, and rogue out any that are not strong and healthy, or that show any undesirable characteristics.

If there is danger of undesirable crosses, cucumbers can be hand-pollinated, using the system described for squash.

It's easy to tell the male from the female blossoms. Each plant will have both. The female or pistillate flowers are not in groups, as are the male or staminate flowers. Beneath the female flower, there is a tiny growth that looks like a small cucumber. This is the ovary.

If you have raised cucumbers, you know there are white-spined varieties, grown for slicing, and black-spined varieties, grown for pickling. The former will be a yellowish-white when mature, while the latter will be much darker, from golden to

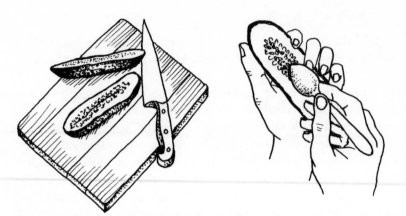

*The four easy steps for saving cucumber seed. First, split the cucumber lengthwise, then, using a spoon, scrape out all of the seeds and the pulp surrounding them.*

brown. Any cucumber that does not follow this rule should not be saved for seed.

I have found that cucumber vines are blackened by the first fall frost, and that this makes selection of cucumbers to be saved for seed an easy task, since suddenly all of the cucumbers are very visible, no longer hidden beneath the green leaves. I select a half-dozen cucumbers from as many plants, and will mix the seeds of all together, even though this will give me far more seeds than I will need. If you have hand pollinated and marked certain cucumbers, these of course will be the ones you use for seed.

Split the cucumber lengthwise, then scrape out the seeds and the pulp surrounding them. A spoon will do the job. Dump this mixture into a large glass bowl, then let it sit and ferment in the kitchen for about five days, stirring it at least once a day, to discourage any mold from forming.

By the end of the five days, most of the seed will have separated from the pulp and will be down at the bottom of the bowl. Retrieve several of them and rub them between your fingers. Their slippery coating has been lost in the fermentation process, you will discover.

*Place the mixture in a bowl to ferment. Stir mixture several times daily to discourage mold. Pulp will become watery, and seeds to save will sink to the bottom. Dry on screen.*

The top layer of pulp and undeveloped seeds can now be removed, leaving the desired seeds at the bottom of the bowl. These can be washed by filling the bowl with water (not hot water), letting the seeds settle to the bottom of the bowl, then pouring off the water.

Spread the seeds on paper towels or a screen, separate them as much as possible, then let them dry, inside or out in the sun. Shake them around occasionally, so that they do not cling together and thus retain moisture.

**MUSKMELON** (*Cucumis melo*). Annual. Monoecius, with separate male and female blossoms. Cross-pollinated by bees.

Growing muskmelons for seed follows most of the instructions for growing cucumbers. There are two major differences:

1. The muskmelon likes warm weather, even more than does the cucumber, and may demand a longer growing season.

2. When the muskmelon is ready to eat, the seeds are mature.

*Muskmelon and its vine.*

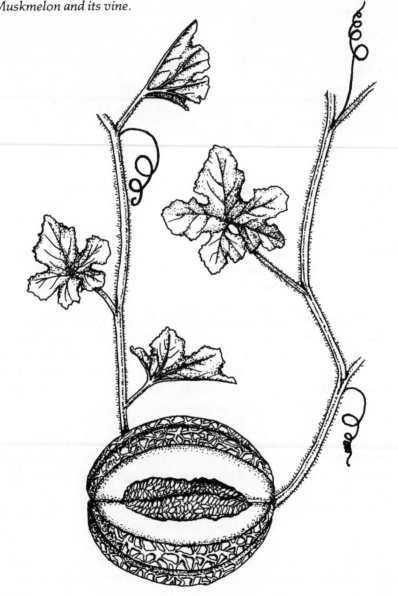

This of course means that the melon can be eaten and enjoyed after the seeds and pulp have been removed.

Follow instructions under cucumber for isolation, roguing, seed production and harvesting, and for separating seeds from the pulp.

**WATERMELON** (*Citrullus vulgaris*). Annual. Monoecius, with separate male and female blossoms. Cross-pollinated by bees.

This melon is grown only in the warmer areas of the country, although the area has pushed northward with the development of new, hardier varieties, and the use of greenhouses to start plants. The watermelon will cross with citron fruit and other varieties of watermelon, but not with muskmelons, cucumbers, squashes, or pumpkins. The ideal isolation distance is a minimum of a quarter mile. Watermelon can be pollinated by hand, as described under squash.

As with muskmelons, the seeds of watermelons are mature when the melon is ready to be eaten. There are several methods that can be used to determine this. One is to check under the watermelon, where it rests on the soil. If this area has turned from white to yellow, the melon should be ripe.

Extracting seeds from watermelon should be a pleasant family effort. The larger the group of participants, the better. Provide several chilled watermelons, cups or bowls for the black seeds, trash containers for the rind. Serve slices of watermelon until all are filled or the desired number of seeds has been obtained. The fastidious will wash these seeds. Dry them well.

For other instructions on growing these seeds, see cucumbers.

# COMPOSITAE

## Composite Family

**LETTUCE** (*Lactuca sativa*). Annual. Perfect flowers, with both male and female parts. Self-pollinating.

Because lettuce is self-pollinating, varieties can be grown in adjacent rows, although to prevent the occasional crossing, it is better to plant another crop between rows of different varieties.

You probably think of lettuce as an early crop, but, in growing for seed, it's a long-season crop.

There are several methods of planting. One is to plant as soon as the soil can be worked, since a frost will not kill the tiny lettuce plants.

Another is to start the seeds indoors, or in a cold frame, then set out the plants about one foot apart. This is an excellent idea for any gardener, assuring him of lettuce to eat at least a month earlier than when the lettuce seed is planted outdoors.

In warmer areas, lettuce is planted in the late fall, and produces seed in the spring.

This same method can be tried in cooler climates for the crisp-head varieties that are slow to bolt and produce seeds. The time of late summer planting will vary geographically, but the gardener should aim for plants about two inches in height when cold weather halts growth. This height has proven to be the level at which least winter damage can be expected. The tiny plants can be mulched after the first heavy frosts to provide protection. The area where they are growing should be well drained. If this method is tried, thinning the plants should be delayed until spring.

Aim for a foot of space between plants when lettuce reaches the bolting stage. If planting is heavier than this, the gardener can remove any plants with undesirable characteristics while thinning.

*Romaine lettuce produces
a tall seed stalk.*

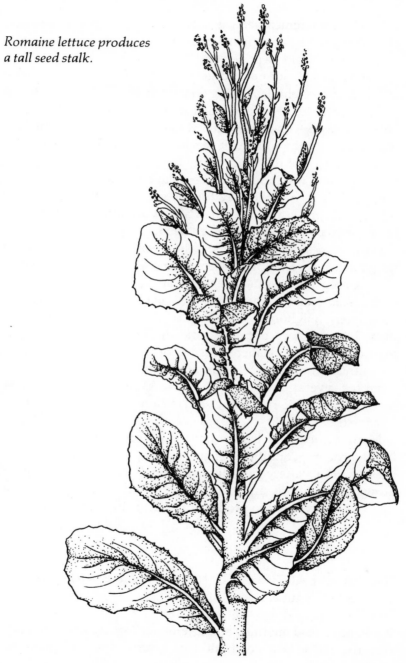

You should remember that early bolting is not a desirable characteristic, so any plants that bolt and produce seed at a record pace should be pulled and the seeds discarded.

The plants will put up seed stems that are from two to five feet tall, with the height depending on the variety.

Some varieties of lettuce, particularly the crisp-heads, should be encouraged to produce seed stalks by cutting an X into the top of the head as soon as it reaches full growth, or by cutting off the top half of the head, or by opening the leaves at the top of the head. This should not be delayed, since the reason for doing this is to free the way for the growth of the stem before it begins its growth, rather than after normal development has been halted by the closely packed head.

Lettuce does not produce seed in a way most convenient for the gardener. The yellow flowers open over a period of a month, and the seeds, presenting a feathery appearance on the branches of the seed stalk, mature over a similar period, about twelve days later. If ignored, this early seed will be lost. Shake the plant into a paper bag any time the seed is seen. This will provide more and cleaner seeds. Another method is to wait for the branches to have a feathery appearance, then cut them. Dry them for several days on a canvas to save any seed that falls, then shake out the remaining seed. Winnow the seed to remove any trash.

Many varieties of lettuce have been produced that do best in the growing conditions of specific areas. The gardener who starts with a variety of lettuce he prefers, who provides good growing conditions and discards any undesirable plants, can improve that variety to produce one best suited for his garden.

**JERUSALEM ARTICHOKE** (*Helianthus tuberosus*). Perennial. Propagated by tubers.

If you have read anything about Jerusalem artichokes, you know that the name is a corruption of words, and the plant has

nothing to do with either Jerusalem or artichokes. It was cultivated by North American Indians, and was a source of pleasure
to the empty stomach of many an early colonist.

Plant tubers four inches deep, two feet apart in rows three
feet apart, and in an area of the garden where the plant, all six
to eight feet of it, will not shade other crops, and where its
missionary zeal toward taking over the entire garden can be
curbed. The tubers do not store well after being dug, so they
should be left in the ground, and dug up, in the fall or early

*Jerusalem artichoke blossom.*

spring, as they are needed for eating or for propagation. This tuber is an excellent vegetable, flavorful and crammed with nutrition. It's easy to grow too; neither pest nor disease has challenged the long line of my Jerusalem artichokes, nor slowed its expanding width. ·

**SALSIFY** (*Tragopogon porrifolius*). Biennial. Perfect flowers, with both male and female parts. Self-pollinating.

Salsify is a delicious root vegetable that has won little popularity. Like parsnip, its taste is improved by cold weather. Even in northern Vermont the roots can be left in the ground during the winter, then dug up for eating in the spring.

If you wish to raise salsify seed, you will carry this one step further, selecting the best of your roots, in the spring, and replanting them a foot apart, in rows three feet apart. And if you do not wish to rogue the plants, simply leave one root every foot as you are harvesting the rest.

In the second year, the salsify plant will grow about three feet tall, with large, purple flowers. When the seeds develop and mature, (with the "feathers" of dandelions), pick the individual heads in the morning, and dry them for several days. Then rub the heads between your hands to free the seeds, and winnow them.

# Further Reading

Readers who desire to read more about seeds should consult the following books:

Cox, J. and G. Starr. *Seed Production and Marketing*. New York and London: John Wiley & Sons, 1927.

Edmond, J. B. *et al.*, *Fundamentals of Horticulture*. New York: McGraw-Hill, 1964.

Hartmann, Hudson and Dale E. Kester. *Plant Propagation*. Englewood Cliffs, N.J.: Prentice-Hall Inc., 1975.

Hawthorn, L.R. and L.H. Pollard. *Vegetable and Flower Seed Production*. New York and Toronto: Plakiston, 1954.

Knott, James Edward. *Handbook for Vegetable Growers*. New York: John Wiley, 1962.

Rickett, Harold William. *Botany for Gardeners*. New York: McMillan Co., 1957.

Weatherwax, Paul. *Indian Corn in Old America*. New York: McMillan Co., 1954.

Whitsin, John *et al.*, eds. *Luther Burbank, His Methods and Discoveries and Their Practical Application*. New York: Luther Burbank Press, 1914.

U.S. Department of Agriculture. *Seeds, Yearbook of Agriculture 1961*. Washington, D.C.: USDA, 1961.

# Glossary for Gardeners

*(Compiled from the 1977 Yearbook of Agriculture)*

**Acclimate**—Plants conditioned or becoming conditioned to a new climate or different growing environment. (See Hardening Off).

**Acid (Sour) Soil**—Soils with a pH below 7; most fruits and vegetables grow best when the pH is between 5.2 to 7.1.

**Alkaline (Sweet) Soil**—Soil with a pH above 7; some fruits and vegetables will grow in mildly alkaline (7.4–8.0) soils, such as asparagus, beans, leeks, okra, grapefruit, lemons.

**Annuals**—Plants living one year or less. During this time the plant grows, flowers, produces seeds, and dies. Examples: beans, peas, sweet corn, squash.

**Axils (leaf)**—The angle or upper side where the leaf is attached to the stem.

**Biennial**—Growing vegetatively during the first year and fruiting and dying during the second.

**Blanching**—Excluding light to reduce the green color or chlorophyll in plants or plant parts, as with celery, Witloof chicory, or cauliflower.

**Bolting**—Production of flowers and seeds by such plants as spinach, lettuce, and radishes, generally occuring when days are long and temperatures warm.

**Broadcast**—Scattering seed or fertilizers uniformly over the soil surface rather than placing in rows.

**Chlorophyll**—Green coloring matter within the cells of plants.

**Chlorosis**—Lack of green color in leaves; may be caused by nutritional deficiencies, environmental conditions, or disease.

**Clone**—A group of plants derived from an individual plant by vegetative propagation such as grafting, cutting, or divisions rather than from seed.

**Clove**—One of a group of small bulbs produced by garlic and shallot plants.

**Cold Frame**—An enclosed, unheated but covered frame useful for growing and protecting young plants in early spring. The top is covered with glass or plastic and located so it is heated by sunlight.

**Compost**—Decayed vegetable matter such as leaves, grass clippings, or barnyard manure. It usually is mixed with soil and fertilizer. Valuable as a mulch in a garden or for improving soil texture, and in potting soils.

**Cool Crops**—Vegetables that do not thrive in summer heat, such as cabbage, English peas, lettuce, or spinach.

**Corm**—Enlarged flesh base of a stem, bulb-like but solid, in which food accumulates. Propagated by division of the cloves. Examples: Dasheen (Taro), garlic, and shallots.

**Cotyledon(s)**—Seed leaf or leaves containing stored food for initial seedling growth.

**Crown (Plant)**—Growing point above the root where the tops or shoots develop as with lettuce, spinach, carrots, celery, and rhubarb.

**Crucifer**—The mustard family. Radishes, cabbage, cauliflower, broccoli, and turnips are members.

**Cucurbit**—The gourd family to which cucumbers, muskmelon, watermelon, pumpkin, and squash belong.

**Cultivar**—This means "cultivated variety" and may be used in place of the word "variety" to indicate a specific horticultural selection.

**Cure**—To prepare for storing by drying the skins. Dry onions and sweet potatoes are typical examples.

**Cutting**—Plant stem including a node that is cut or snapped off and used to start a new plant.

**Damping Off**—A disease causing seedlings to die soon after germination, either before or after emerging from the soil.

**Determinate Tomato**—Stem growth stops when the terminal bud becomes a flower bud. Tomato plants of this type are also known as self-topping or self-pruning.

**Division**—Propagation of plants by cutting them into sections as is done with plant crowns, rhizomes, stem tubers, and tuberous roots. Each section must have at least one head or stem. Example: Rhubarb.

**Drill Row**—Small planting furrow made with a hoe, trowel, stick or mechanical drill in which seeds are planted.

**Everbearing**—Plants such as strawberries which bloom intermittently and thus produce fruit during the entire growing season.

**Fertilization**—(1) Union of pollen with the ovule to produce seeds. This is essential in production of edible flower parts such as tomatoes, squash, corn, strawberries, and many other garden plants. (2) Application to the soil of needed plant nutrients, such as nitrogen, phosphate, and potash.

**Flat**—Shallow wooden or plastic box, in which vegetable seeds may be sown or cuttings rooted.

**Foot-candle**—Standard measure of light. The light of one candle falling on a surface one foot away from the candle.

**Friable (Soil)**—Generally refers to a soil that crumbles when handled. A loam soil with physical properties that provide good aeration and drainage, easily tilled. Friable condition is improved or maintained by annual applications of organic matter.

**Fumigation**—Control of insects, disease-causing organisms, weeds, or nematodes by gases applied in an enclosed area such as a greenhouse or under a plastic cover laid on the garden soil.

**Fungicide**—A pesticide chemical used to control plant diseases caused by fungi such as molds and mildew. (See Pesticide).

**Furrow**—Small V-shaped ditch made for planting seed or irrigating. (See Drill Row).

**Germination**—Sprouting of a seed, and beginning of a plant growth.

**Greens**—Vegetables such as spinach, kale, collards, turnip greens.

**Growing Medium**—Soil or soil substitute prepared by combining such materials as peat, vermiculite, sand, or weathered sawdust. Used for growing potted plants or germinating seed.

**Growing Season**—Period between last killing frost in spring and first killing frost in fall.

**Hardening Off**—Adapting plants to outdoor conditions by withholding water, lowering the temperature, or gradually eliminating the protection of a cold frame, hot bed, or greenhouse. This conditions plants for survival when transplanted outdoors.

**Hardy Plants**—Plants adapted to winter temperatures or other climatic conditions of an area. Half hardy indicates some plants may be able to take local conditions with a certain amount of protection.

**Herbaceous Plant**—Plants that die back to the ground each winter, such as asparagus and rhubarb.

**Hill**—Raising the soil in a slight mound for planting, or setting plants some distance apart.

**Host Plant**—Plant on which an insect or a disease-causing organism lives.

**Hot Caps**—Waxpaper cones, paper sacks, cardboard boxes or plastic jugs with bottoms removed placed over individual plants in spring for frost and wind protection.

**Hotbed**—Same type of structure as a cold frame but heated, as with an electric cable.

**Humus**—Decomposed organic material that improves texture and productive qualities of garden soils.

**Hydroponics**—Growing plants in nutrient solutions rather than soil. Also called soilless gardening.

**Hybrid $F_1$**—Plants of a first generation hybrid of two dissimilar parents. Hybrid vigor, insect or disease resistance, and uniformity are qualities of this generation. Seed from hybrid vegetables grown in your garden should not be saved for future planting. Their vigor and productive qualities are only in the original hybrid seed.

**Immune**—Free from disease infection because of resistance. Not subject to attack by a specified pest. Immunity is absolute.

**Indeterminant Tomato**—Terminal bud is always vegetative, thus the stem grows indefinitely. Indeterminant plants can be trained on a trellis, a stake, or in wire cages. (See Determinate Tomato).

**Indigenous**—Native to a particular region. Opposite of exotic.

**Inflorescence**—Entire floral structure of a plant.

**Inoculation**—Treatment of seed with bacteria that stimulate development of bacteria nodules on plant roots. Used on legumes such as peas and beans.

**Insecticide**—Chemicals or agents used to control insects either on contact or as a stomach poison.

**Internode**—Region on a plant system between the nodes.

**Interplanting**—Getting maximum production from a garden by planting early maturing vegetables between rows of slow maturing vegetables. An example is radishes or onions between rows of sweet corn.

**Irrigation**—Applying water to the soil by sprinklers, trickle or flooding.

**K**—Symbol for potash.

**Layering**—Way of propagating plants vegetatively. A stem is bent down and buried in a rooting medium to induce root development along the buried portion.

**Leggy**—Weak-stemmed and spindly plants with sparse foliage caused by too much heat, shade, crowding, and over-fertilization.

**Legume**—Plant that takes nitrogen from air with the nitrifying bacteria that live on its roots. Examples are garden peas and beans.

**Lifting**—Digging a plant for replanting or winter storage.

**Light Soil**—Soil that is easy to cultivate, retains little moisture, and has sandy or coarse texture.

**Lime**—Compound containing calcium and/or magnesium, applied to soils to reduce acidity.

**Loam**—Soil that consists of less than 52% sand, 28% to 50% silt, and 7% to 27% clay, resulting in a soil texture ideal for gardening.

**Manure**—Animal waste used as soil conditioner and fertilizer.

**Micro-climate**—Climate of a small area or locality as compared to a country or state. For example, the climate adjacent to the north side of a home, or influence of a lake on a portion of a county.

**Micro-organism**—Any microscopic animal or plant that may cause a plant disease or have the beneficial effect of decomposing plant and animal residue that becomes humus.

**Mildew**—Plant disease caused by several fungi, recognized by the white cottony coating on plants.

**Mist**—Applying vaporized water to cuttings in the propagating stage.

**Mites**—Extremely small sucking insects that infest various plants.

**Monoecious**—Plants that have male and female sex organs in different flowers on the same plant, such as cucumbers and squash.

**Mulch**—Materials such as straw, leaves, lawn clippings, sawdust, black plastic sheets, or newspapers laid on the soil surface to conserve moisture, maintain an even soil temperature, and control weeds.

**Nematode**—Microscopic, worm-like, transparent organism that can attack plant roots or stems to cause stunted or unhealthy growth.

**Nitrogen**—One of plant nutrients essential for growth and green color in plants. Available in both organic and inorganic forms. Designated by the letter N.

**Nitrogen Fixation**—Transformation of nitrogen from the air into nitrogen compounds by nitrifying bacteria on the roots of legumes.

**NPK**—Symbols for three of primary nutrients needed by plants. N is for nitrogen, P for phosphate, K for potash or potassium. Percentage of these nutrients in a fertilizer package is always listed in that order.

**Node**—Region of a plant stem that normally produces leaves and buds.

**P**—Symbol for phosphate.

**Parasite**—Plant or insect that attaches itself to another organism and obtain food from the host. Dodder is an example of a parasite plant.

**Parthenogenic**—Fruit produced without fertilization of the ovule(s). Usually seedless. (See Fertilization 1).

**Patented**—Plant varieties protected by a government patent, granting exclusive rights to the patent holder.

**Peat or Peat Moss**—Partially decomposed plant life taken from bogs and used as rooting medium, soil conditioner, or mulch.

**Peat Pot**—Made of compressed peat and often used for starting and growing plants that can be later planted in the garden without removing the pot.

**Perennials**—Any plant which normally lives more than two years. Examples are artichoke, asparagus, raspberry, and rhubarb.

**Perlite**—Volcanic or silica material expanded by heat treatment. Used as a soil amendment and in media for rooting cuttings. (See Rooting Media).

**Pesticide**—General term for any chemical used to control pests.

**pH**—Chemical symbol used to give relative acidity or alkalinity of the soil. The scale ranges from 0 to 14, with 7 the neutral reading. Readings of less than 7 indicate acid soil, readings above indicate alkaline soil.

**Phosphate**—One of the three major nutrients, designated by the letter P.

**Photoperiod**—Length of the light period in a day.

**Photoperiodism**—Effect of differences in length of light period upon plant growth and development.

**Pinching**—Removing the terminal bud or growth to stimulate branching.

**Plant Food**—See Plant Nutrient.

**Plant Nutrient**—Substance or ingredient furnishing nourishment and promoting growth in plants. Examples: nitrogen, phosphorous, potassium, iron and sulfur supplied by the soil, organic matter and fertilizers.

**Plant Variety Protected**—Plant varieties protected by the Government plant variety law granting exclusive rights to the holder.

**Plunge**—To cover or sink a plant container to the rim in sawdust, soil, peat moss, or similar materials.

**Pollen**—Reproductive material, usually dust-like, produced by male part of a flower.

**Pollination, Open**—Transfer of pollen from flower of one plant to flower of the same or different plant by natural means.

**Pollination, Self**—Transfer of pollen from male part of one flower to female part of the same flower, or to another flower on the same plant.

**Potash**—One of three major plant nutrients essential for plant growth. Same as potassium. Designated by letter K.

**Pot-bound**—Plants whose roots completely fill a container and surround the soil ball in which they are growing, restricting normal top growth of the plant.

**Pot Herb**—Plants grown or used for greens.

**Potting Mixture**—Combination of soil and other ingredients such as peat, sand, perlite, or vermiculite designed for starting seed or growing plants in containers.

**Propagation**—Increasing the number of plants by planting seed or by vegetative means from cuttings, division, grafting, or layering.

**Resistance**—Ability of a plant to restrict disease or insect damage or withstand severe climatic conditions.

**Respiration**—Chemical process by which the plant absorbs oxygen from the air and releases water and carbon dioxide into the air.

**Rest Period**—Normal period of inactivity in growth of plant.

**Rhizome**—Horizontal underground stem distinguished from a root by the presence of nodes and internodes and buds and scale-like leaves.

**Rogue**—Off-type or diseased plant. Or removal of such plants from the garden.

**Root-bound**—When plants have grown in a container too long. The roots become a mass of fibers and no longer support desired top growth. Same as pot-bound.

**Root Crop**—Vegetables grown for their edible roots, such as beets, carrots, radishes and turnips.

**Rooting Media**—Materials such as peat, sand, or vermiculite in which cuttings are placed during the development of roots.

**Runner**—Slender, elongated and prostrate branch that has buds and can form roots at the nodes or at the tip. An example is a strawberry runner.

**Seed Bed**—Garden soil after it has been prepared for planting seeds or transplants by plowing and disking, rototilling, spading or raking.

**Seed Leaves**—See Cotyledon.

**Seedling**—Young plant developing from a germinating seed. It usually has the first true leaves developed.

**Sets**—Small onion bulbs used for early planting.

**Short Season Vegetables**—Vegetables ready for harvest after one to two months following planting.

**Sidedressing**—Applying fertilizer on soil surface close enough to a plant so cultivating or watering would carry the fertilizer to the plant's roots.

**Silt**—Soil particles that are between sand and clay in size.

**Slips**—Same as "cutting." A way of vegetatively propagating plants.

**Softwood Cutting**—Cutting taken from a woody or herbaceous plant before it has matured.

**Soil**—Upper layer of the earth's surface, composed of organic matter, minerals, and micro-organisms, and capable of supporting plant life.

**Soil Sterilization**—Treating soil by fumigation, chemicals, heat or steam to destroy disease-causing organisms.

**Soil Texture**—Proportional amounts of sand, silt, clay, and organic matter in a given soil.

**Sour Soil**—Same as an acid soil or one that has a pH below 7. See pH.

**Specimen Plant**—A plant with some outstanding quality such as flowers, leaves, fruit, or branching habit and located as a focal point in the landscape.

**Sphagnum**—Mosses which grow in bogs and when decomposed become peat moss.

**Spreader**—Materials added to pesticide sprays to aid in distribution and coverage of the plant. Can also mean the mechanism used for spreading seed and fertilizers on the soil.

**Staking**—Tying plants such as tomatoes to a stake to provide support.

**Starter Solution**—Fertilizer solution applied to plants at time of transplanting.

**Stolon**—Slender, prostrate subterranean stem. It may produce a tuber such as a potato.

**Stress (Water)**—Plant(s) unable to absorb enough water to replace that lost by transpiration. Results may be wilting, halting of growth, or death of the plant or plant parts.

**Susceptible**—Inability of plants to restrict activities of a specified pest, or to withstand an adverse environmental condition.

**Syringe**—Applying a mist-like spray to seedlings or transplants to reduce or replace moisture lost by transpiration.

**Tamping**—Lightly firming soil over seeds or around newly set transplants.

**Tankage**—Fertilizer prepared from slaughterhouse refuse that has been sterilized and pulverized.

**Tendril**—Slender twining organ found along stems of some plants such as grapes, whch helps the vine to both climb and cling to a support.

**Thinning**—Removing small or young plants from a row to provide remaining plants with more space to grow and develop.

**Till**—To prepare and use land for crop or plant growth by plowing, fertilizing and cultivating.

**Tilth**—Physical condition of a soil. "Good tilth" indicates soil has right proportions of sand, silt, clay, and organic matter so it is easily worked or cultivated.

**Tolerant**—Ability of plants to endure a specified pest or an adverse environmental condition, growing and producing despite the disorder.

**Topdressing**—Applying materials such as fertilizer or compost to the soil surface while plants are growing.

**Trace Elements**—Minerals such as boron, manganese, iron or zinc normally required only in small amounts by plants. Also known as "minor elements."

**Transplanting**—Digging up a plant and moving it from one location to another.

**Transpiration**—Loss of water through openings called *stomata* on the leaves of plants.

**Trenching**—Deep digging of garden soil and mixing in compost, manure, or some other soil conditioner.

**True Leaf**—An ordinary leaf, which functions in the production of food by a plant.

**Tuber (Stem)**—Thickened or swollen underground branch or stolon with numerous buds or eyes. Thickening occurs because of the accumulation of reserved food. Example: A potato or Jerusalem artichoke.

**Tuberous Roots**—Thickened roots, differing from stem tubers in that they lack nodes and internodes, and buds are present only at the crown or stem end. Example: Sweet potato.

**Variety**—Closely related plants forming subdivision of a species and having similar characteristics. (See Cultivar).

**Vegetative Growth**—Growth of stems and foliage on plants as opposed to flower and fruit development.

**Vegetative Propagation**—Increasing the number of plants by such methods as cuttings, grafting, or layering.

**Vermiculite**—A mica product expanded by heat, forming a lightweight soil additive. Often used in synthetic soil mixes or as a rooting medium for cuttings.

**Viable**—Alive, such as seed capable of germinating.

**Virus**—Pathogenic organism too small to be seen with a compound microscope but capable of causing plant diseases. Often spread from infected to healthy plants by sucking insects such as aphids or thrips, or through pruning or handling of plants.

**Wettable Powders**—Pesticide blended with a filler and wetting agent to permit mixing with water.

**Wetting Agent**—Material incuded in pesticide solutions that reduces surface tension and helps to completely cover the surface or foliage area of the plant being sprayed. (See Spreader.)

**Wilting**—Drooping of leaves and stems due to lack of water. Can result from root damage, disease, injury, or hot drying winds.

**Windrow**—Hay, grain, leaves, etc. swept or raked into rows to dry.

# Other Garden Way Books
# You Will Enjoy

*Down-to-Earth Vegetable Gardening Know-How*, featuring Dick Raymond, 160 pages, deluxe illustrated paperback, $5.95. Special durable cover edition, $7.95. A treasury of complete vegetable gardening information.

*Keeping the Harvest: Home Storage of Vegetables & Fruits*, by Nancy Thurber and Gretchen Mead. 208 pages, deluxe illustrated paperback, $5.95; hardcover, $9.95. The very best of the food storage books.

*Profitable Herb Growing at Home*, by Betty E.M. Jacobs. 240 pages, quality paperback, $5.95. The perfect book for those who wish to expand a home herb garden into a money-making country sideline.

*What Every Gardener Should Know About Earthworms*, by Dr. Henry Hopp. 40 pages, quality paperback, $1.50. The benefits of earthworms in making richer soils and bigger crops.

*Secrets of Companion Planting for Successful Gardening*, by Louise Riotte. 226 pages, quality paperback, $5.95, hardcover, $8.95. For bigger, more luscious crops.

*Let It Rot!*, by Stu Campbell. 152 pages, quality paperback, $3.95. Homemade fertilizers for a healthier garden.

These books are available at your bookstore, or may be ordered directly from Garden Way Publishing, Department 171X, Charlotte, VT 05445. If order is less than $10, please add 60¢ postage and handling.